BRAIN GAMES™

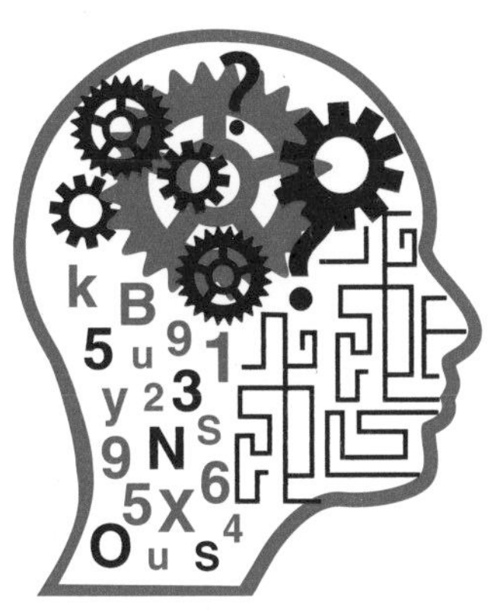

Consultant: Elkhonon Goldberg, Ph.D.

Publications International, Ltd.

Elkhonon Goldberg, Ph.D., ABPP/ABCN, (consultant) is a clinical professor of neurology at New York University School of Medicine, a diplomate of the American Board of Professional Psychology/American Board of Clinical Neuropsychology, and director of The East-West Science and Education Foundation. Dr. Goldberg created the Manhattan-based Cognitive Enhancement Program, a fitness center for the brain, and he is author of the international best-selling books *The Wisdom Paradox: How Your Mind Can Grow as Your Brain Grows Older* and *The Executive Brain: Frontal Lobes and the Civilized Mind.*

Julie K. Cohen is a puzzle developer, puzzle consultant, author, and freelance writer. She has published numerous math puzzle books, and her puzzles for children and adults appear in national magazines, Web sites, puzzle books, cellular phone games, and DVDs. To learn more about Cohen, visit her Web site, http://www.JulieKCohen.com.

Amy Reynaldo, the author of *How to Conquer the New York Times Crossword Puzzle*, created the first crossword blog (Diary of a Crossword Fiend) and reviews 1,500 crosswords a year. She is a top-10 finisher at the American Crossword Puzzle tournament.

Puzzle Constructors: Michael Adams, Cihan Altay, Myles Callum, Philip Carter, Kelly Clark, Barry Clarke, Conceptis Puzzles, Don Cook, Mark Danna, Harvey Estes, Josie Faulkner, Adrian Fisher, Erich Friedman, Peter Grabarchuk, Serhiy Grabarchuk, Ray Hamel, Luke Haward, Marilynn Huret, Steve Karp, Lloyd King, Dan Meinking, Kate Mepham, David Millar, Michael Moreci, Dan Moore, Elsa Neal, Alan Olschwang, Dave Roberts, Marylin Roberts, Stephen Ryder, Gianni Sarcone, Pete Sarjeant, Paul Seaburn, Fraser Simpson, Terry Stickels, Howard Tomlinson, Wayne Robert Williams

Illustrators: Helem An, Nicole H. Lee, Elizabeth Gerber, Shavan R. Spears, Jen Torche

Cover Puzzles: Don Cook, Josie Faulkner, Steve Karp, Pete Sarjeant

Louis Weber, CEO
Publications International, Ltd.
7373 North Cicero Avenue
Lincolnwood, Illinois 60712

ISBN-13: 978-1-4127-4546-8
ISBN-10: 1-4127-4546-2

Manufactured in China.

8 7 6 5 4 3 2 1

CONTENTS

BRAIN FITNESS

Your mind is your most important asset—more important than your house, your bank account, and your stock portfolio. You insure your house and work hard to pad your bank account. But what can you do to sharpen your mind and protect it from decline? With the baby boomer generation getting on in years, an increasing number of people are asking this question. Modern-day science provides a clear answer: Protect your mind by protecting your brain. To understand this relationship further, we turn to cutting-edge research.

Protect and Enhance Your Brainpower

Modern-day neuroscience has established that our brain is a far more plastic organ than was previously thought. In the past it was believed that an adult brain could only lose nerve cells (neurons) and couldn't acquire new ones. Today we know that new neurons—and new connections between neurons—continue to develop throughout our lives, even well into advanced age. This process is called *neuroplasticity*. Thanks to recent scientific discoveries, we also know that we can harness the powers of neuroplasticity in protecting and even enhancing our minds at every stage of life—including our advanced years.

How can we harness neuroplasticity to help protect and enhance our mental powers? Recent scientific research demonstrates that the brain responds to mental stimulation much like muscles respond to physical exercise. In other words, you have to give your brain a workout. The more vigorous and diverse your mental life—and the more you welcome mental challenges—the more you will stimulate the growth of new neurons and new connections between them. Furthermore, the *nature* of your mental activities influences *where* in the brain this growth takes place. The brain is a very complex organ with different parts in charge of different mental functions. Thus, different cognitive challenges exercise different components of the brain.

How do we know this? We've learned this by experiments created from real-life circumstances and *neuroimaging*, the high-resolution technologies that allow scientists to study brain structure and function with amazing precision. Some say that these technologies have done for our understanding of the brain what the invention of the telescope has done for our understanding of the planetary systems. Thanks to these technologies, particularly MRI (magnetic resonance imaging), we know that certain parts of the brain exhibit an increased size in those who use these parts of the brain more than most people. For example, researchers found that hippocampi, the parts of the brain critical for spatial memory, were larger than usual in London cab drivers who have to navigate and remember complex routes in a huge city. Studies revealed that the so-called Heschl's gyrus, a part of the temporal lobe of the brain involved in processing music, is larger in professional musicians than in musically untrained people. And the angular gyrus, the part of the brain involved in language, proved to be larger in bilingual individuals than in those who speak only one language.

What is particularly important—the size of the effect, the extent to which the part of the brain was enlarged—was directly related to the *amount of time* each person spent in the activities that rely on the part of the brain in question. For instance, the hippocampal size was directly related to the number of years the cab driver spent on the job, and the size of Heschl's gyrus was associated with the amount of time a musician devoted to practicing a musical instrument. This shows that cognitive activity directly influences the structures of the brain by stimulating the effects of neuroplasticity in these structures, since the enlargement of brain regions implies a greater than usual number of cells or connections between them. The impact of cognitive activity on the brain can be great enough to result in an actual increase in its size! Indeed, different parts of the brain benefit directly from certain activities, and the effect can be quite specific.

Diversify Your Mental Workout

It is also true that any more or less complex cognitive function—be it memory, attention, perception, decision making, or problem solving—relies on a whole network of brain regions rather than on a single region. Therefore, any relatively complex mental challenge will engage more than one part of the brain, yet no single mental activity will engage the whole brain.

This is why the diversity of your mental life is key to your overall brain health. The more vigorous and varied your cognitive challenges, the more efficiently and effectively they'll protect your mind from decline. To return to the workout analogy: Imagine a physical gym. No single exercise machine will make you physically fit. Instead, you need a balanced and diverse workout regimen.

You have probably always assumed that crossword puzzles and sudoku are good for you, and they are. But your cognitive workout will benefit more from a greater variety of exercises, particularly if these exercises have been selected with some knowledge of how the brain works.

The puzzle selection for *Brain Games*™ has been guided by these considerations—with knowledge of the brain and the roles played by its different parts in the overall orchestra of your mental life. We aimed to assemble as wide a range of puzzles as possible in order to offer the brain a full workout.

There is no single magic pill to protect or enhance your mind, but vigorous, regular, and diverse mental activity is the closest thing to it. Research indicates that people engaged in mental activities as a result of their education and vocation are less likely to develop dementia as they age. In fact, many of these people demonstrate impressive mental alertness well into their eighties and nineties.

What's more, the pill does not have to be bitter. You can engage in activities that are both good for your brain *and* fun. Different kinds of puzzles engage different aspects of your mind, and you can assemble them all into a cognitive workout regimen. Variety is the name of the game—that's the whole idea! In any single cognitive workout session, have fun by mixing puzzles of different kinds. This book offers you enough puzzle variety to make this possible.

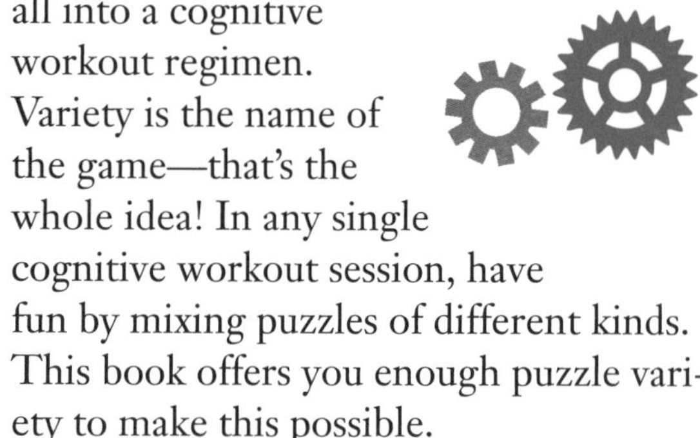

Welcome challenging puzzles, instead of feeling intimidated by them. Never give up! To be effective as a mental workout, the puzzles should not be too easy or too difficult. An overly easy puzzle will not stimulate your brain, just as a leisurely walk in the park is not an efficient way to condition your heart. You need mental exertion. On the other hand, an overly difficult puzzle will just frustrate and discourage you from moving forward. So it is important to find the "challenge zone" that is appropriate for you. This may vary from person to person and from puzzle to puzzle. Here too, the gym analogy applies. Different people will benefit most from different exercise machines and from different levels of resistance and weights.

With this in mind, we have tried to offer a range of difficulty for every puzzle type. Try different puzzles to find the starting level appropriate to you. And before you know it, your puzzle-cracking ability will improve, your confidence will grow, and this will be a source of reassurance, satisfaction, and even pride.

Have Fun While Stretching Your Mind

The important thing is to have fun while doing something good for you. Puzzles can be engaging, absorbing, and even addicting. An increasing number of people make regular physical exercise part of their daily routines and miss it when circumstances prevent them from exercising. These habitual gym-goers know that strenuous effort is something to look forward to, not to avoid. Similarly, you will strengthen your mental muscle by actively challenging it. Don't put the puzzle book down when the solution is not immediately apparent. By testing your mind you will discover the joy of a particular kind of accomplishment: watching your mental powers grow. You must have the feeling of mental effort and exertion in order to exercise your brain.

This brings us to the next issue. While all puzzles are good for you, the degree of their effectiveness as brain conditioners is not the same. Some puzzles only test your knowledge of facts. Such puzzles may be enjoyable and useful to a degree, but they're not as useful in conditioning your brain as the puzzles that require you to transform and manipulate information or do something with it by logic, multistep inference, mental rotation, planning, and so on. The latter puzzles are more likely to give you the feeling of mental exertion, of "stretching your mind," and they are also better for your brain health. You can use this feeling as a useful, though inexact, assessment of a puzzle's effectiveness as a brain conditioner.

Try to select puzzles in a way that complements, rather than duplicates, your job-related activities. If your profession involves dealing with words (e.g., an English teacher), try to emphasize spatial puzzles. If you are an engineer dealing with diagrams, focus on word puzzles. If your job is relatively devoid of mental challenges of any kind, mix several types of puzzles in equal proportions.

Cognitive decline frequently sets in with aging. It often affects certain kinds of memory and certain aspects of attention and decision making. So it is particularly important to introduce cognitive exercise into your lifestyle as you age to counteract any possible cognitive decline. But cognitive exercise is also important for the young and the middle-aged. We live in a world that depends increasingly on the brain more than on brawn. It is important to be sharp in order to get ahead in your career and to remain at the top of your game.

How frequently should you exercise your mind and for how long? Think in terms of an ongoing lifestyle change and not just a short-term commitment. Regularity is key, perhaps a few times a week for 30 to 45 minutes at a time. We've tried to make this easier by offering a whole series of *Brain Games*™ books. You can carry these puzzle books—your "cognitive workout gym"—in your briefcase, backpack, or shopping bag. Our puzzles are intended to be fun, so feel free to fit them into your lifestyle in a way that enhances rather than disrupts it. Research shows that even a relatively brief regimen of vigorous cognitive activity often produces perceptible and lasting effects. But as with physical exercise, the results are best when cognitive exercise becomes a lifelong habit.

To help you gauge your progress, we have included two self-assessment questionnaires: one on page 9, and the other on page 166. The questionnaires will guide you in rating your various cognitive abilities and any change that you may experience as a result of doing puzzles.

Try to be as objective as possible when you fill out the questionnaires. Improving your cognitive skills in real-life situations is the most important practical outcome of exercising your mind, and you are in the best position to note such improvement and to decide whether or not it has taken place.

Now that you're aware of the great mental workout that awaits you in this book, we hope that you'll approach these puzzles with a sense of fun. If you have always been a puzzle fan, we offer a great rationale for indulging your passion! You have not been wasting your time by cracking challenging puzzles—far from it; you have been training and improving your mind.

So, whether you are a new or seasoned puzzle-solver, enjoy your brain workout and get smarter as you go!

ASSESS YOUR BRAIN

You are about to do something very smart: embark on a set of exercises to improve the way your mind works. The puzzles assembled in this book are fun and they have been selected to hone your memory, attention, problem-solving, and other important mental skills. So before you begin, we would like you to fill out a brief questionnaire. It is for your own benefit, so you know how your mind worked before you challenged it with our exercises. This will allow you to decide in the future if any change in your mental performance has taken place and in what areas.

The questions below are designed to test your skills in the areas of memory, problem-solving, creative thinking, attention, language, and more. Please take a moment to think about your answers and rate your responses on a 5-point scale, where 5 equals "excellent" and 1 equals "very poor." Then tally up your scores, and go to the categories at the bottom of the next page to see how you did.

1. You get a new cell phone. How long does it take you to remember the number? Give yourself a 1 if you have to check the phone every time you want to give out the number and a 5 if you know it by heart the next day.

   1 2 3 4 5

2. How good are you at remembering where you put things? Give yourself a 5 if you never lose anything but a 1 if you have to search for the keys every time you want to leave the house.

   1 2 3 4 5

3. You have a busy work day that you've carefully planned around a doctor's appointment. At the last minute, the doctor's office calls and asks you to reschedule your appointment from afternoon to morning. How good are you at juggling your plans to accommodate this change?

   1 2 3 4 5

4. You're taking a trip back to your hometown and have several old friends to see, as well as old haunts to visit. You'll only be there for three days. How good are you at planning your visit so you can accomplish everything?

   1 2 3 4 5

5. A friend takes you to a movie, and the next morning a curious coworker wants to hear the plot in depth. How good are you at remembering all the details?

   1 2 3 4 5

6. Consider this scenario: You're brokering an agreement between two parties (could be anything from a business merger to making peace between feuding siblings), and both parties keep changing their demands. How good are you at adapting to the changing situation?

   1 2 3 4 5

7. You're cooking a big meal for a family celebration. Say you have to cook everything—appetizers, entrees, sides, and desserts—all on the same day. How good are you at planning out each recipe so that everything is done and you can sit down and enjoy the meal with your family?

   1 2 3 4 5

8. In an emotionally charged situation (for example, when you're giving a toast), can you usually come up with the right words to describe your feelings?

   1 2 3 4 5

9. You and five friends have made a vow to always spend a certain amount of money on each other for holiday gifts. How good are you at calculating the prices of things in your head to make sure you spend the right amount of money?

   1 2 3 4 5

10. You're moving, and you have to coordinate all the details of packing, hiring movers, cutting off and setting up utilities, and a hundred other small details. How good are you at planning out this complex situation?

    1 2 3 4 5

10–25 Points: Are You Ready to Make a Change?
Remember, it's never too late to improve your brain health! A great way to start is to work puzzles each day, and you've taken the first step by buying this book. Choose a different type of puzzle each day, or do a variety of them to help strengthen memory, focus, attention, and improve logic and problem-solving.

26–40 Points: Building Your Mental Muscle
You're no mental slouch, but there's always room to sharpen your mind! Choose puzzles that will challenge you, especially the types of puzzles you might not like as much or wouldn't normally do. Remember, doing a puzzle can be the mental equivalent of doing lunges or squats: While they might not be your first choice of activities, you'll definitely like the results!

41–50 Points: View from the Top
Congratulations! You're keeping your brain in tip-top shape. To maintain this level of mental fitness, keep challenging yourself by working puzzles every day. Like the rest of the body's muscles, your mental strength can decline if you don't use it. So choose to keep your brain supple and strong. You're at the summit, now you just have to stay to enjoy the view!

GET YOUR MIND GOING

LEVEL 1

ABCD

LOGIC PLANNING

Every cell in this grid contains 1 of 4 letters: A, B, C, or D. No letter can be horizontally or vertically adjacent to itself. The tables above and to the left of the grid indicate how many times each letter appears in that column or row. Can you complete the grid?

			A	2	0	1	1	1	0
			B	2	2	2	2	0	2
			C	0	3	3	2	2	3
A	B	C	D	2	1	0	1	3	1
0	2	3	1				C		
1	3	2	0						
1	0	3	2						
1	1	1	3						
2	2	2	0						
0	2	2	2						

Spell Math!

ANALYSIS COMPUTATION

Spell out numbers in the blanks below to obtain the correct solution. Numbers are used only once and range from 1 to 20. A letter has been given to get you started.

___ ___ ___ ___ ___ + ___ ___ v ___ ___ = ___ ___ ___

Answers on page 168.

Codeword

ANALYSIS LANGUAGE

Each letter of the alphabet is hidden in code: They are represented by a random number from 1 through 26. With the letters already given, complete the crossword puzzle with common English words and break the code.

2	6	23	26	15		23	11	16	7	23	14	16
6		16		1		10			2		16	
17		2		11		22		12	14	8	14	18
23	15	15	2	4	9	2	2		19		26	
4		22		22		5		12	2	4	3	23
18	14	4	21	1	26	23	11		11			4
14		2		15				9		9		14
24			20		23	13	1	23	11	14	1	10
2	18	15	2	11		1		18		24		22
	13		15		7	14	21	7	4	2	18	18
4	1	11	18	2		16		14		11		14
	23		23			7		4		15		15
23	15	22	10	14	25	2		21	23	18	18	3

A B C D E F G H I J K L M N O P Q R S T U V W X Y Z

1	2	3	4	5	6	7	8	9	10	11	12	13
U			N									

14	15	16	17	18	19	20	21	22	23	24	25	26
		C										

Answer on page 168.

Word-a-Maze: On the Go

CREATIVE THINKING | GENERAL KNOWLEDGE

Travel in sequence through the puzzle from the left side to the right, using each numbered clue to determine the correct word. Connect adjacent words together with a common letter to proceed through the maze. Some letters are already given. The first and last words tie into the title.

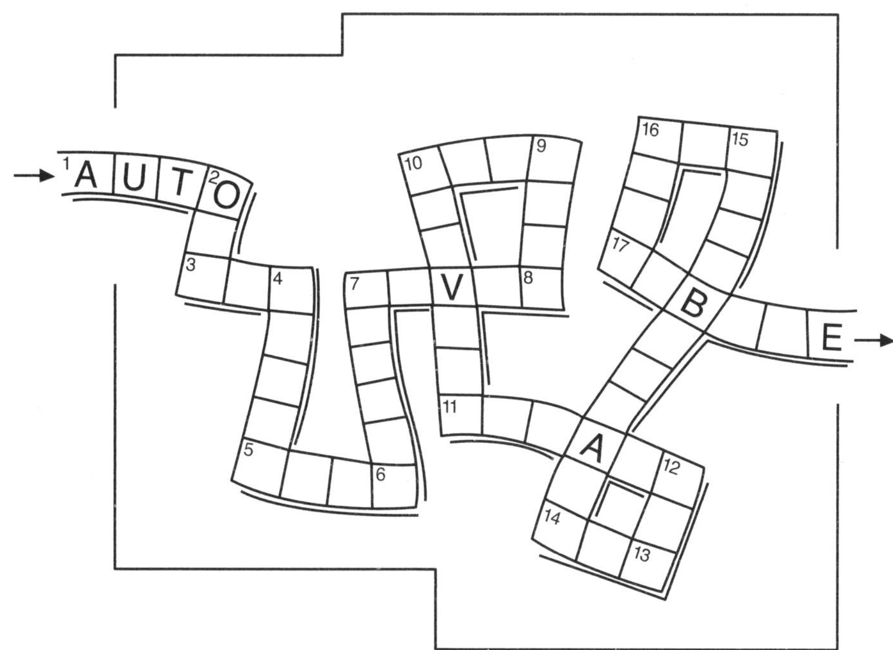

1. Biography beginning
2. Business assn.
3. Choke
4. Trial answer
5. Look for
6. Type of roll
7. Amazon, for one
8. Spool
9. Quantity of bread
10. "Model T"
11. Draw parallel
12. ________ of corn
13. Spoil
14. One way to get there
15. Tell on
16. Haircut
17. Crib decoration

Answers on page 168.

The "T" Sound

ATTENTION | VISUAL SEARCH

Every word listed below is contained within this group of letters. Words can be found horizontally, vertically, or diagonally. They may read either backward or forward. Leftover letters tell what "T is for" according to an old song.

```
M E E T S E T I C A N T E E N
S F O T S Q U A R E T E A S E
R T H R E T T O T R E T E E T
E T E A R A S S K H S E S H E
          D C A T T
          S E H E T
          T O A E S
          E M A N R
          E V P Y H
          P Y R B T
          R T E O E
          E N T P E
          E U T P T
          T O Y E E
          S C M R E
```

CANTEEN	STEAM	TEAK	TEETH
COUNTY	STEEP	TEASE	T-SQUARE
ESTEEM	STEER	TEENY-BOPPER	
PRETTY	TEACHER	TEETER-TOTTER	

Hidden song quote: ______________________________

Answers on page 168.

Battle Boats

ANALYSIS LOGIC

Place each ship in the fleet located at right within the grid. Ships may be placed horizontally or vertically, but they don't touch each other, not even diagonally. Numbers reveal the ship segments located in that row or column.

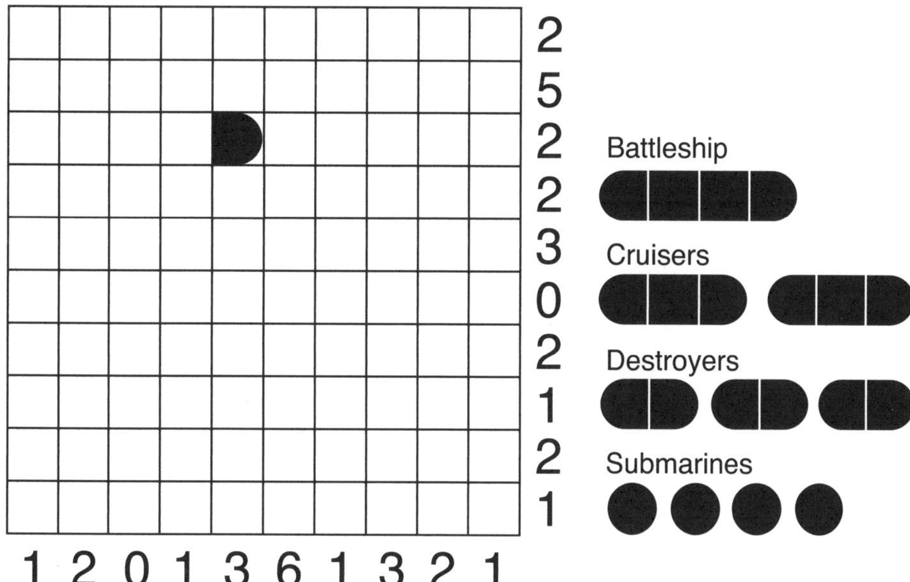

Famous Anagrams

LANGUAGE

Below are anagrams of 4 famous figures. Which one is NOT an anagram for a famous cartoon character?

A. Old dank cud

B. Yum ice smoke

C. True rump chord

D. Snub by gnu

Answers on page 168.

It's Magic!

GENERAL KNOWLEDGE | LANGUAGE

1	2	3	4	■	5	6	7	8	■	9	10	11
12				■	13				■	14		
15				16					17			
18					■	■	19					
■	■	■	20		21	■	■	22			■	■
23	24	25	■	26		27	28	■	29		30	31
32			33					34				
35				■	36				■	37		
■	■	38		39	■	■	40		41	■	■	■
42	43				44	■	■	45		46	47	48
49						50	51					
52			■	53				■	54			
55			■	56				■	57			

ACROSS

1. Fish eggs
5. Meat roasting rod
9. Program guide abbr.
12. Othello's treacherous adviser
13. Model anew
14. She sits on eggs
15. Titania
18. Ear related
19. Wolflike
20. ________-mo (instant replay speed)
22. Slalom curve
23. RCA products
26. ________ mater
29. Italian volcano
32. What bubbled in a cauldron in "Macbeth"
35. ________-Day Vitamins
36. Staircase unit
37. Weep
38. Big biblical boat
40. Fr. holy woman

42. Actress Dahl
45. Slur over a syllable
49. Dorothy and Toto sought him
52. "...________ the land of the free..."
53. Head: Fr.
54. Couple
55. Dads
56. Timetable, for short
57. "At Last" blues singer James

DOWN

1. Actress Hayworth
2. Where Pearl Harbor is
3. River through Bavaria
4. Couch potatoes' hangouts
5. ________ Lanka
6. Each
7. Pastoral poem
8. Brimless bonnet
9. Like one believing in God
10. "________ there, done that"
11. Henry VIII's second wife
16. Supreme Being in Islam
17. Like a capsized canoe... or its rower
21. Bullfight cheers
23. Tango necessity?
24. Coq au ________ (chicken in wine)
25. Thieves
27. Colorado hrs.
28. Tarzan's buddies
30. Neither's partner
31. "________ takers?"
33. Baseball Hall-of-Famer Rod
34. Chose
39. Makes booties, maybe
41. Wed on the run
42. Resting on
43. Flightless South American bird
44. Book before Daniel: abbr.
46. "________ first you don't succeed..."
47. "Let's ________" (Cole Porter song)
48. Poet Pound
50. Had a bite
51. Traffic light color

Answers on page 168.

1-2-3

LOGIC PLANNING

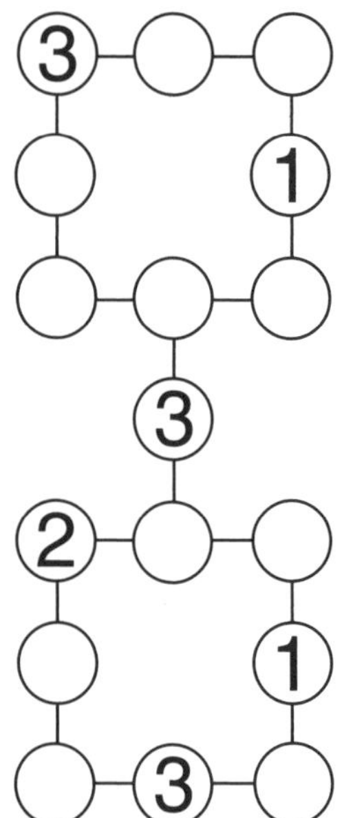

Place the numbers 1, 2, and 3 in the circles below. The challenge is to have only these 3 numbers in each connected row and column—no number should repeat. Any combination is allowed.

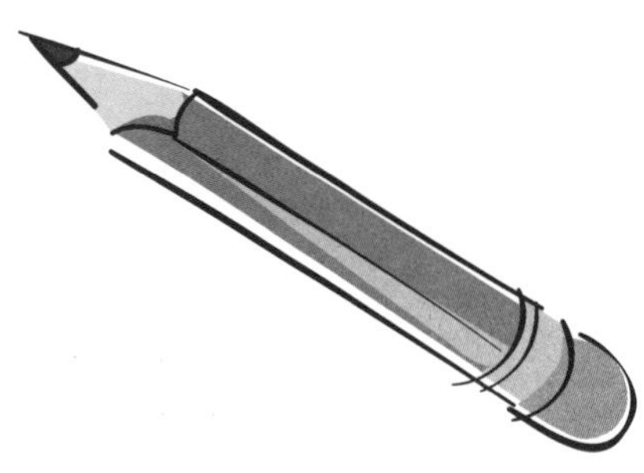

Crypto-Logic

COMPUTATION LOGIC

Each of the numbers in the sequence below represents a letter. Use the mathematical clues to determine which number stands for which letter and reveal the encrypted word.

4931

Clues:

S = 5	S − T = N
2S = I	N − A = T
I ÷ 10 = T	3A = E

Answers on page 169.

Try Your Luck

PLANNING SPATIAL REASONING

Don't get too caught up in all the twists and turns as you find your way out of this slot machine.

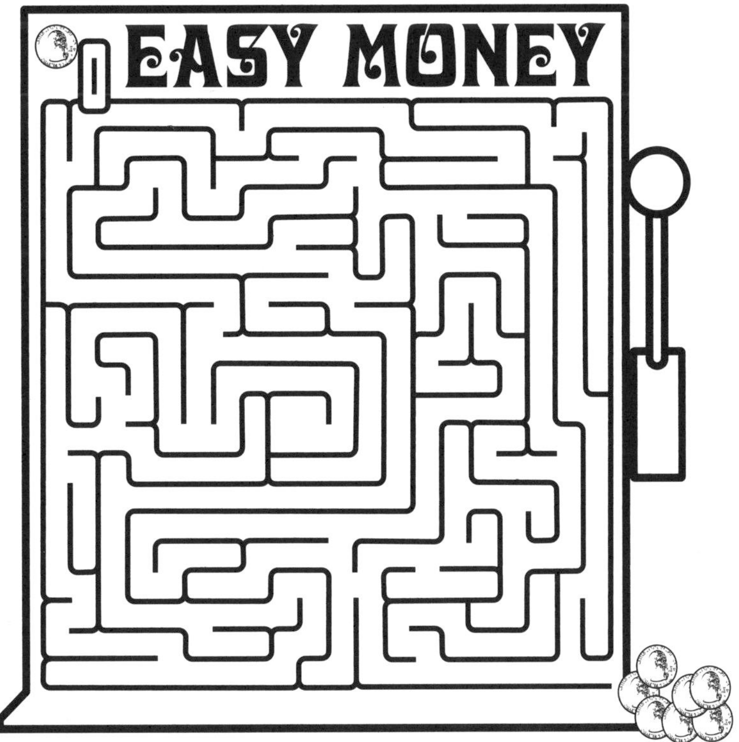

Say What?

CREATIVE THINKING LANGUAGE

Below are a group of words that, when properly arranged in the blanks, reveal a quote from George Orwell.

joke mental a dirty rebellion

"A ________ ________ is ________ sort of ________ ________."

Answers on page 169.

Shenanigans

ANALYSIS VISUAL LOGIC

A rebus follows its own type of alphabet: a mixture of letters, symbols, and pictures. Look carefully at the rebus below. You should be able to "read" the solution to the clue given in the title.

Fitting Words

GENERAL KNOWLEDGE PLANNING

In this miniature crossword, the clues are listed randomly and are numbered for convenience only. It is up to you to figure out the placement of the 9 answers. To help you, we've inserted one letter in the grid, and this is the only occurrence of that letter in the completed puzzle.

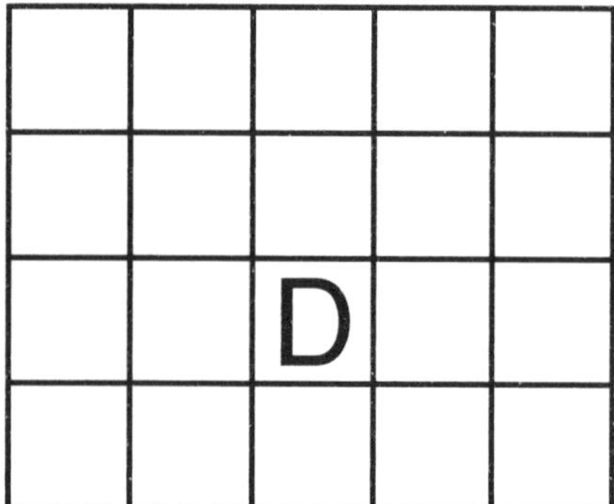

Clues

1. Carbonated drinks
2. ________ browns (breakfast potatoes)
3. Third rock from the sun
4. Burn soother
5. Molars or incisors
6. Went by subway
7. Hawaiian hello
8. Not this
9. Sunrise direction

Answers on page 169.

Ring-Around-a-Rosie

CREATIVE THINKING | GENERAL KNOWLEDGE

The arrows indicate the beginning space for each 6-letter word. Each word circles its number in a clockwise direction.

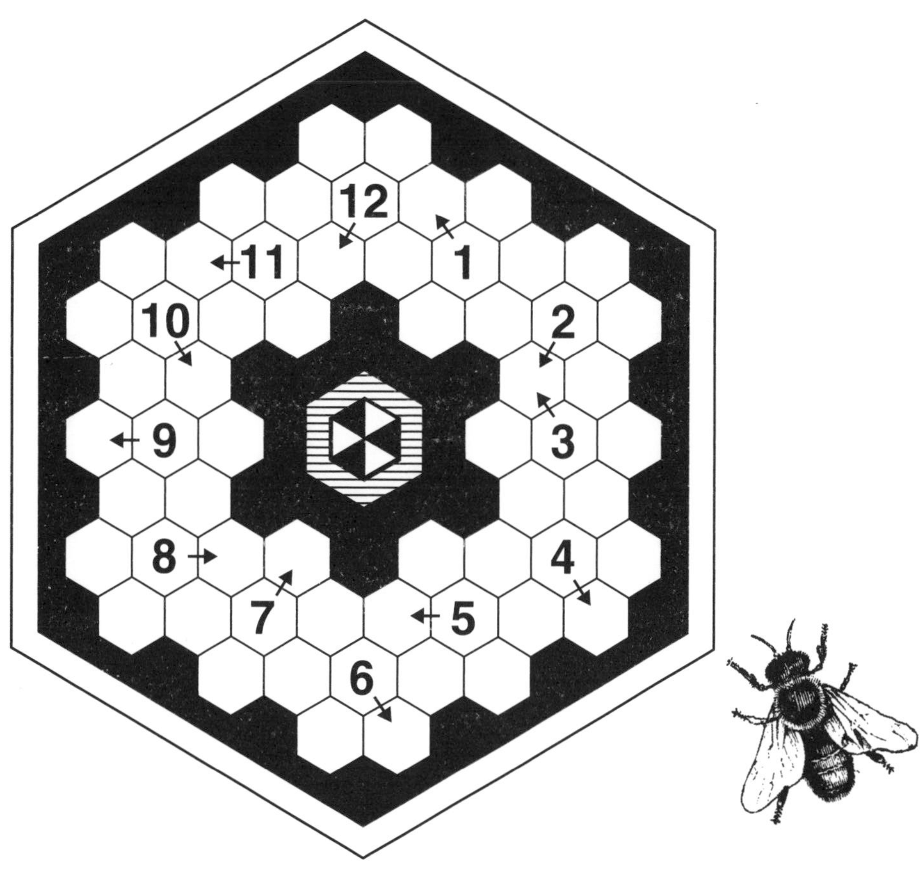

1. Cut in a record
2. First-year player
3. Mend
4. Lasso
5. Homecoming event
6. Harsh, grating sound
7. One who tills the soil
8. Say from memory
9. Stemmed glass
10. Home of the Celtics
11. Western state
12. Washington or Burns

Answers on page 169.

L'adder

ANALYSIS | COMPUTATION

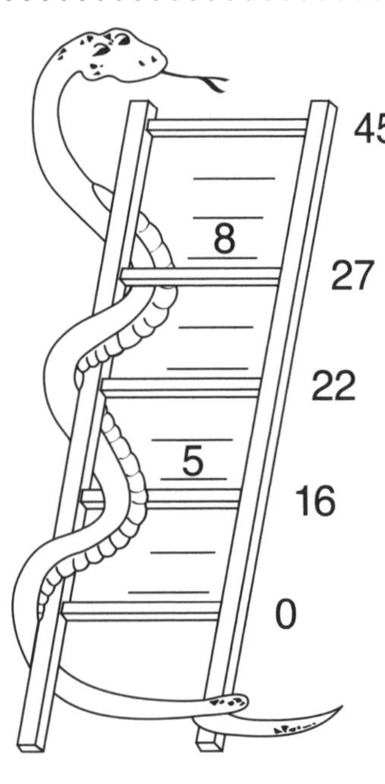

Starting at the bottom rung, use the numbers 1 through 9 to add up to the top number. Numbers can only be used once. There's a catch though: The precise sums must be met along the way.

Dissection

CREATIVE THINKING | SPATIAL VISUALIZATION | VISUAL LOGIC

Separate the figure into 2 identical parts following the grid lines. The parts may be rotated and/or mirrored.

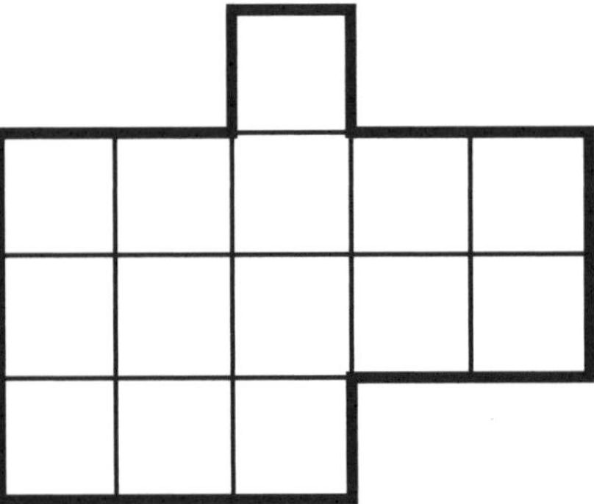

Answers on page 169.

Word Ladder

LANGUAGE PLANNING

Use the clues to change just one letter on each line to go from the top word to the bottom word. Do not change the order of the letters. You must have a common English word at each step.

BALL

________ to become pale

________ put milk in it

________ it hurts

________ chess piece

YAWN

Code-doku

LANGUAGE LOGIC

					S		E	R
S						K		F
C								
R		C				P	K	
			K					
	F		I					
P		E		S		C		
K			N		P			I
		N	C	E				

Solve this puzzle just as you would a sudoku. Use deductive logic to complete the grid so that each row, column, and 3 by 3 box contains the letters from the words PICK FERNS. When you have completed the puzzle, read the shaded squares from left to right and top to bottom to reveal a hidden message.

Hidden message: ______________________

____

Answers on page 169.

Bee-Bop Jive

ATTENTION | VISUAL SEARCH

Only 1 bee looks the same after an hour of serious bee-bop. Can you find it?

Trivia on the Brain

Researchers say one of the best ways to improve your mood is to count your blessings and to visualize your best possible future self.

Answer on page 170.

Elevator Words

GENERAL KNOWLEDGE | LANGUAGE

Like an elevator, words move up and down the "floors" of this puzzle. Starting with the first answer, the second word from each answer carries down to become the first word of the following answer. With the clues given, complete the puzzle.

1. 747, for one	1. Jumbo ______
2. Personal water craft	2. ______ ______
3. Ride up the snow-covered slope	3. ______ ______
4. Roadside rescue vehicle	4. ______ ______
5. A place for refueling on the highway	5. ______ ______
6. Street light alternative	6. ______ ______
7. Communication using hand gestures	7. ______ Language

Vex-a-Gon

CREATIVE THINKING | PLANNING

Place the numbers 1 through 6 into the triangles of each hexagon. The numbers may be in any order, but they do not repeat within each hexagon shape.

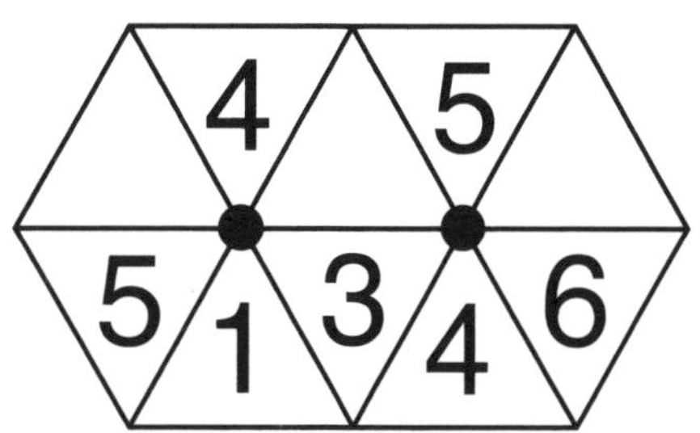

Answers on page 170.

Crossed Words

LANGUAGE

Unscramble the letters in each line to solve the puzzle. The words cross on a letter that they both use.

Clue: As different as…

```
      S
  K H C L A
      H
      E
      E
      E
```

Cross Sums

COMPUTATION PLANNING

Use the numbers below to fill in the grid. Each cell at the top of the 3 adjacent cells is the sum of numbers below it. So, as seen in the example, A=B+C+D.

1 2 3 4 6 7 10 11 14 15 28 40 101

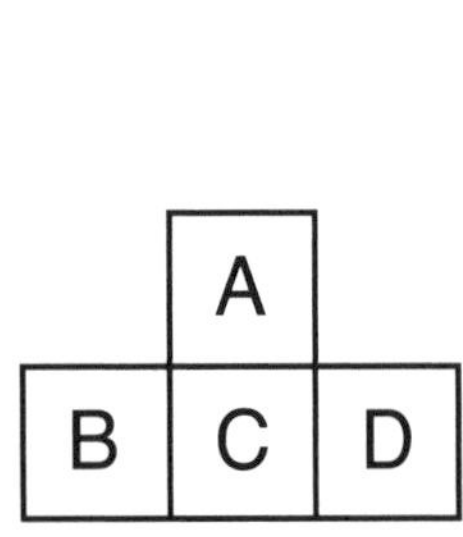

			☐			
		☐	33	☐		
	☐	☐	☐	7	☐	
☐	☐	5	☐	☐	☐	☐

Answers on page 170.

Hashi

PLANNING VISUAL LOGIC

Each circle represents an island, with the number inside indicating the number of bridges connected to it. Draw bridges between islands using the number given. There can be no more than 2 bridges going in the same direction and there must be a continuous path connecting all islands. Bridges can only be vertical or horizontal and may not cross islands or other bridges. We've drawn some bridges to get you started.

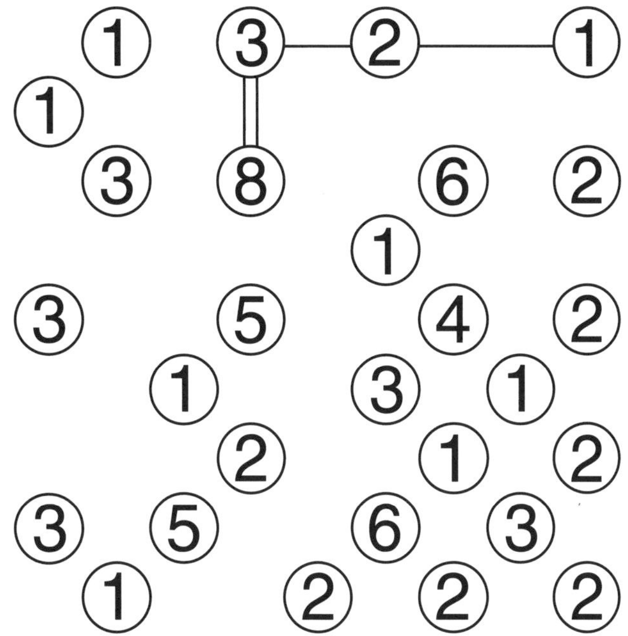

Trivia on the Brain

Before electricity was invented, the average adult got about 8.5 hours of sleep a night. Today, the average adult gets 6.9 hours of sleep. But we still need just as much sleep as they did, even though we can turn night into day with a flip of a switch.

Answer on page 170.

We, the Jury by Alpha Sleuth™

LANGUAGE PLANNING

Move each of the letters below into the grid to form common words. You will use each letter once. The letters in the numbered cells of the grid correspond to the letters in the phrase at the bottom. Completing the grid will help you complete the phrase and vice versa. When finished, the grid and phrase will be filled with valid words and you will have used all the letters in the letter set.

Hint: The numbered cells in the grid are arranged alphabetically, so the letter in the cell marked 1 will appear in the alphabet before the letter in the cell marked 2, and so on.

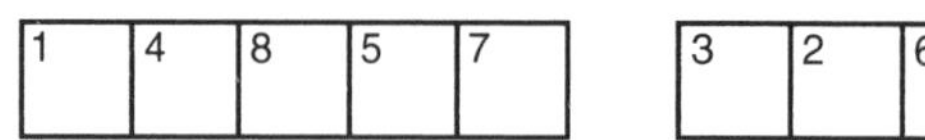

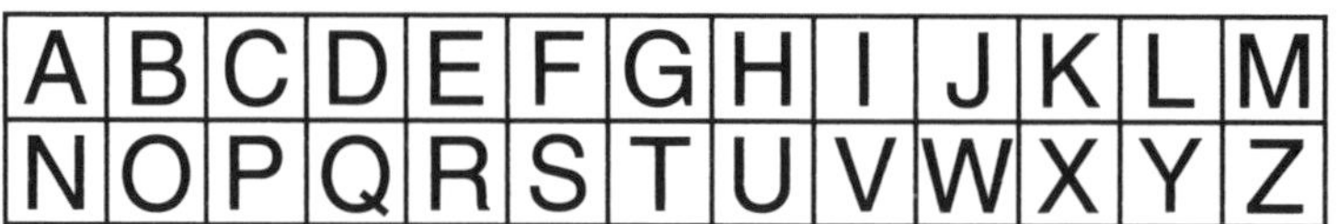

Answer on page 170.

Calcu-doku

COMPUTATION **LOGIC**

Use arithmetic and deductive logic to complete the grid so that each row and column contains the numbers 1 through 4 in some order. Numbers in each outlined set of squares combine to produce the number in the top corner using the mathematical sign indicated. The solution is unique.

7+	6×	1	2×
		2/	
3-			1-
2	4+		

Arrow Web

ANALYSIS **LOGIC**

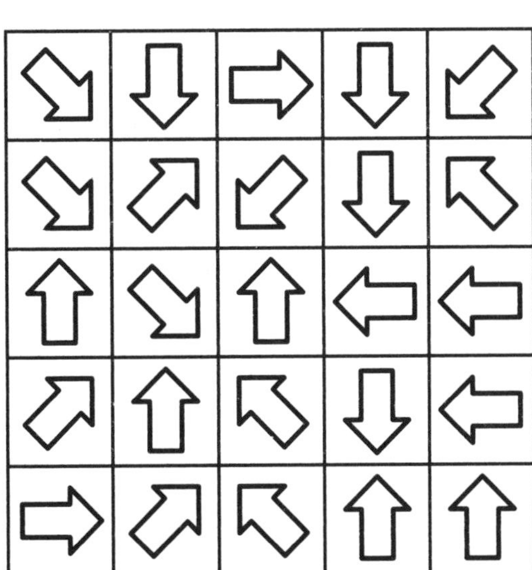

Shade in some of the arrows so that each arrow in the grid points to exactly 1 shaded arrow.

Answers on page 170.

XOXO

ANALYSIS VISUAL LOGIC

Place either an X or an O inside each empty cell of the grid so that there appears no row, column, or diagonal with 4 consecutive cells with the same letter.

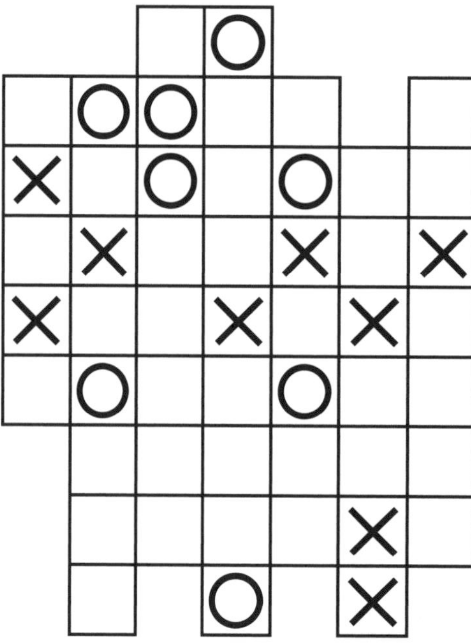

Word Jigsaw

LANGUAGE PLANNING

Fit the pieces into the frame to form common words reading across and down. There's no need to rotate the pieces; they'll fit as shown, with each piece used once.

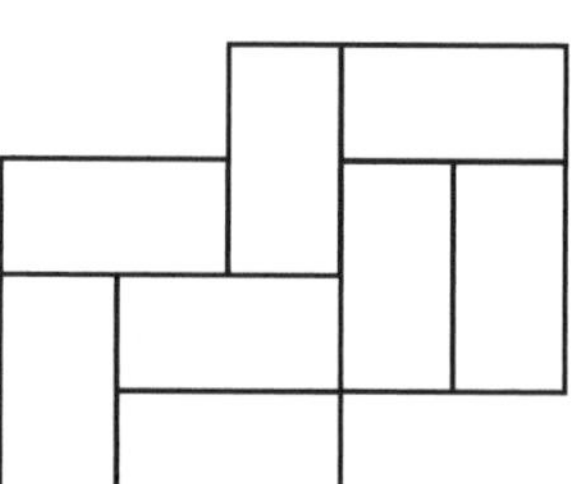

Answers on page 170.

Name Calling

ANALYSIS

Decipher the encoded word in the quip below using the numbers and letters on the phone pad. Remember that each number can stand for 3 or 4 possible letters.

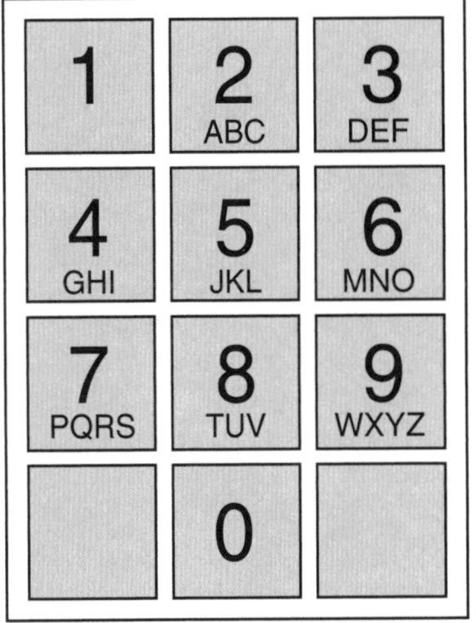

5–2–8–4–4–4–6–4 stock: cattle with a sense of humor

Cluster

ANALYSIS COMPUTATION

Fill in each grape so the number in descending rows is the total of the neighboring numbers from the row above it. Each grape contains a positive whole number. Numbers can be repeated.

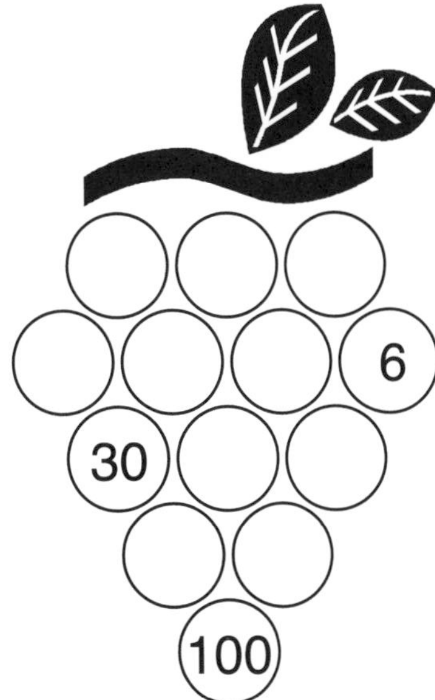

Answers on page 171.

Short Sequence

ANALYSIS CREATIVE THINKING

Determine the next letter that will complete this sequence.

C, D, H, ___

Fit It

ANALYSIS PLANNING

Use each of the names found below to complete the clue-less crossword grid on the following page. The puzzle has only 1 solution.

4 letters
Ford

5 letters
Nixon

Tyler

6 letters
Hoover

Wilson

7 letters
Clinton

Lincoln

9 letters
Cleveland

10 letters
Eisenhower

George Bush

James K. Polk

11 letters
James Monroe

12 letters
Ronald Reagan

13 letters
Ulysses S. Grant

Zachary Taylor

14 letters
Calvin Coolidge

Warren G. Harding

15 letters
James Earl Carter

John Quincy Adams

Millard Fillmore

Thomas Jefferson

16 letters
Benjamin Harrison

George Washington

17 letters
Chester Alan Arthur

Theodore Roosevelt

William Howard Taft

Answer on page 171.

Trivia on the Brain

According to Hermann Ebbinghaus, the 19th-century German psychologist who developed the Ebbinghaus Curve of Forgetting, the average adult forgets 56 percent of newly learned material immediately, 66 percent within a day, and 80 percent within a month.

Answer on page 171.

Star Power

LOGIC PLANNING

Fill in each empty square in the grid so that each star is surrounded by the numbers 1 through 8 with no repeats.

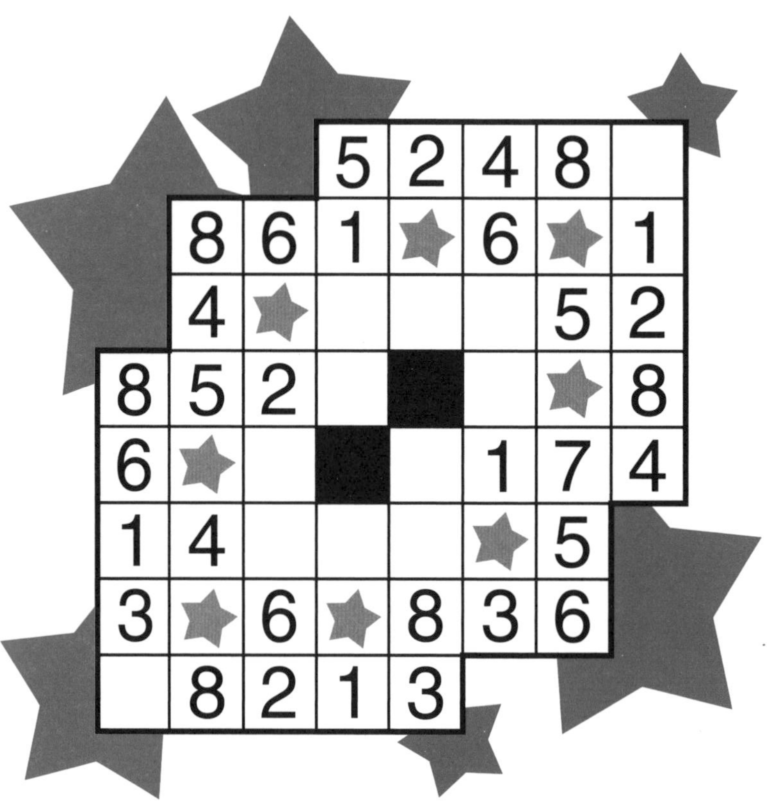

Trivia on the Brain

A *tangram* is a puzzle that creates pictures using 7 shapes—5 triangles, a square, and a parallelogram. One legend claims that it was invented when a man named Tan dropped a porcelain tile that broke into 7 pieces. As Tan tried putting the tile back together, the 7 pieces kept forming different objects and animals.

Answer on page 171.

Cross-Math

COMPUTATION **PLANNING**

Place the digits 1 through 9 in the empty white squares so that the 3 horizontal and 3 vertical equations are true. Each digit will be used exactly once. Calculations are done from left to right and from top to bottom.

	-		+		=	9
+		+		-		
	+		×		=	18
+		+		-		
	+		×		=	26
=		=		=		
17		15		3		

Word Ladder

LANGUAGE **PLANNING**

Use the clues to change just one letter on each line to go from the top word to the bottom word. Do not change the order of the letters. You must have a common English word at each step.

KETTLE

_______ what you're made of

_______ it'll sting you

_______ to get all comfortable

PESTLE

Answers on page 171.

Rhyme Time

GENERAL KNOWLEDGE | LANGUAGE

Each clue leads to a 2-word answer that rhymes, such as BIG PIG or STABLE TABLE. The numbers in parentheses after the clue give the number of letters in each word. For example, "cookware out of the oven (3, 3)" would be "hot pot."

1. Went on a winning streak (3, 3): ________________
2. Rejection by a Chicago team (3, 4): ________________
3. Plumbing problem (4, 4): ________________
4. You complete it for college housing (4, 4): ________________

5. More elegant cruise ship (5, 5): ________________
6. Earthquake cause (4, 5): ________________
7. Silt research (5, 5): ________________
8. Get to the shore (5, 5): ________________

9. Unexpected sharp market decline (5, 5): ________________
10. Majestic raptor (5, 5): ________________

Trivia on the Brain

According to researchers, the number 8 is the easiest number to remember. That's why toll-free phone numbers start with the "800" or "888" prefixes.

Answers on page 171.

Kakuro

ANALYSIS COMPUTATION

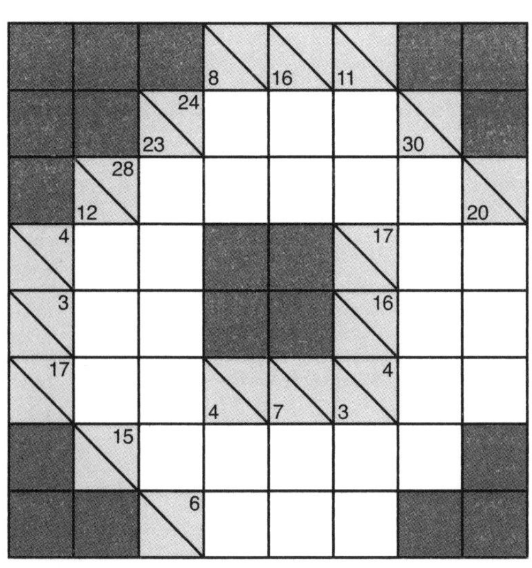

Place a number from 1 through 9 in each empty cell so that the sum of each vertical or horizontal run (rows and columns extending from already numbered cells) equals the number at the top or on the left of that run. Numbers may not be repeated in any run, and runs end at dark-colored squares.

Network

ANALYSIS LOGIC

Enter letters into the empty circles so that the given word can be spelled out in order from letter to consecutive letter through connected circles. Letters can be used more than once.

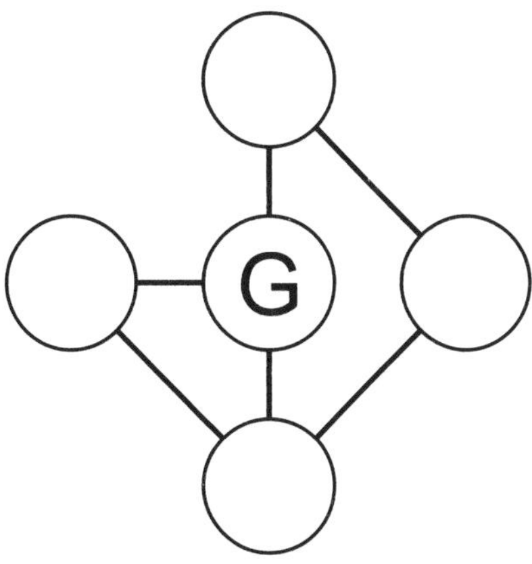

GENESIS

Answers on page 171.

Code-doku

LANGUAGE LOGIC

Solve this puzzle just as you would a sudoku. Use deductive logic to complete the grid so that each row, column, and 3 by 3 box contains each of the letters BDEGHINRU. When you have completed the puzzle, unscramble the letters to reveal the home of the military tattoo in the United Kingdom.

Answer: ______________________

	H	E		B		R		
		D		G				I
N			I				E	H
D	N				I			
		I	D	H	E			R
		H	G				I	B
G					B	H		U
R				I	D			
		B		N		I		

Perfect Score

COMPUTATION VISUAL LOGIC

Make 3 successful hits so that the sum of the numbers is 100. Double and triple scores do not apply. Numbers may be used more than once.

Answers on page 172.

Monetary Scramblegram

LANGUAGE

Four 6-letter words, all of which revolve around the same theme, have been jumbled. Unscramble each word, and write the answer in the accompanying space. Next, transfer the letters that are in the shaded boxes into the shaded keyword space below, and unscramble the 8-letter word that goes with the theme. The theme for this puzzle is international currency.

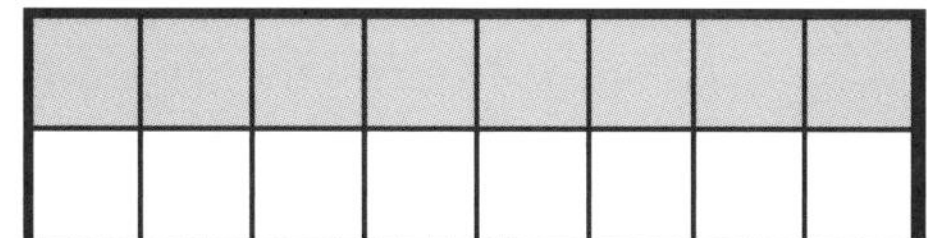

Trivia on the Brain

Canadian Paul Gallant took jigsaw puzzles to another dimension when he introduced 3-D puzzles in 1991. Now, instead of assembling a flat image, people can build skyscrapers in their own home.

Answer on page 172.

Eavesdropping Logic

ANALYSIS LOGIC

You overhear the following comment about a situation between some friends:

"When they heard the news, Dave and Paul agreed that nothing more could have been done, but one could see Paul was less disappointed. Sofia didn't agree with Dave, but she was more frustrated than either with the result."

From this passage, what can't we gather?

A. That Dave had higher hopes for the situation than Paul.

B. That Dave and Paul have different attitudes to how the situation was handled.

C. That Sofia agreed more with Paul than Dave.

D. There are 2 of these 3 things that we can't gather from the passage.

Missing Connections

LANGUAGE PLANNING

It's a crossword without the clues! Use the letters below to fill in the empty spaces in the crossword grid. When you are finished, you'll have words that read both across and down, crossword-style.

A A C D D E K K L M O O P P P

R R R S S S T T T W Y Y Z

Answers on page 172.

Fences

ANALYSIS LOGIC

Connect the dots and draw a continuous path that doesn't cross itself. Numbers represent the "fences" created by the path (2 edges are created around the number 2, 3 edges around 3, etc.). We've started the puzzle for you.

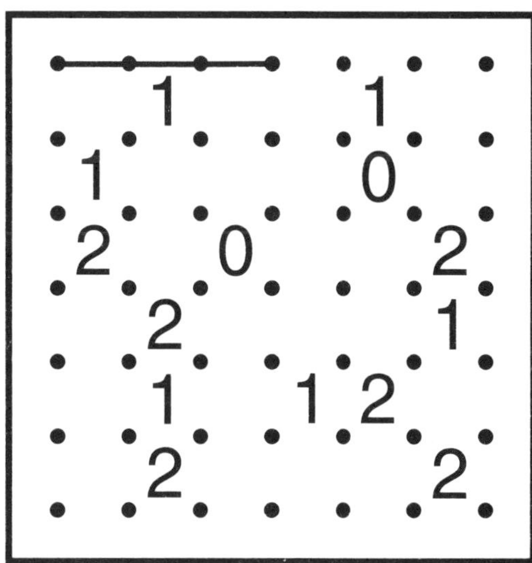

Twenty-four Jumble

ANALYSIS COMPUTATION

Arrange the numbers and signs in this cornucopia to come up with the number 24.

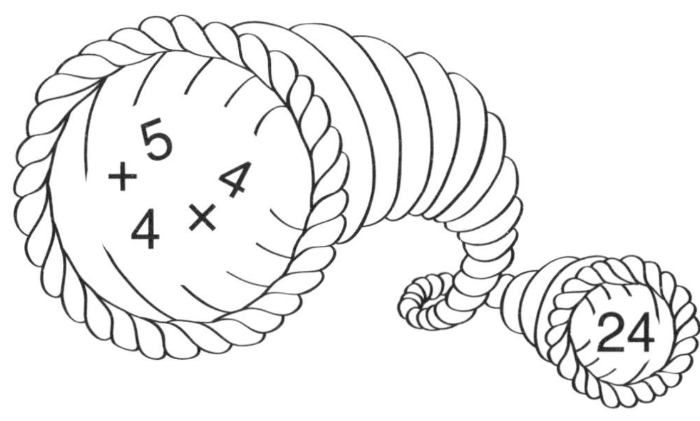

Answers on page 172.

TONE YOUR MENTAL MUSCLE

LEVEL 2

Black Diamonds

COMPUTATION LOGIC

Place the numbers 1 through 4 in the cells of each of the squares below. There's a catch though: Overlapping squares must add up to the number given in each of the black diamonds.

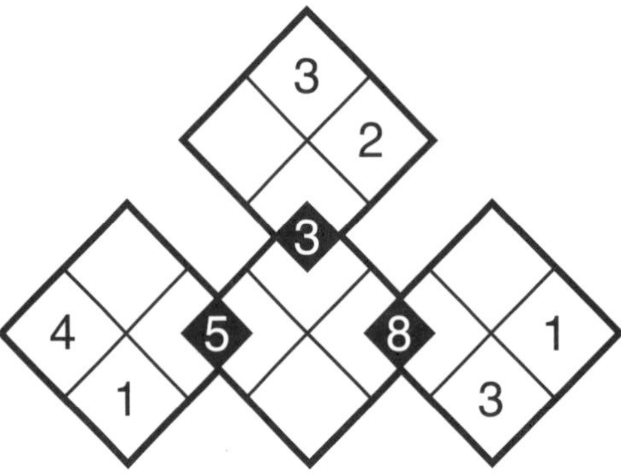

Marbles

ANALYSIS LOGIC

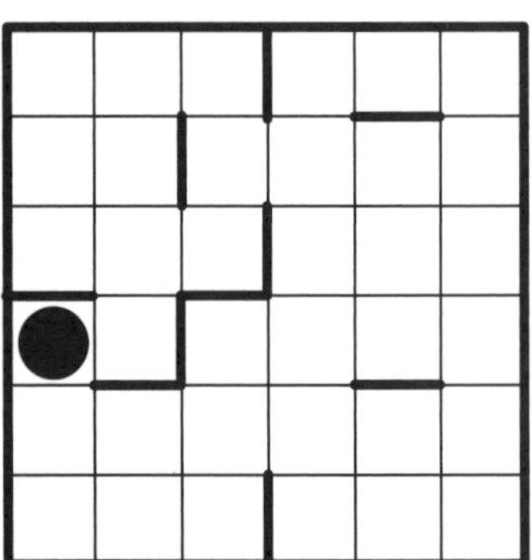

Place 9 marbles into the grid without having any touch one another, not even diagonally. There are some walls, represented by thick lines, that block the view of the marbles. Marbles must not "see" each other in a horizontal or vertical direction. We've placed the first 1 to get you started.

Answers on page 172.

May the Force Be With You

ATTENTION | VISUAL SEARCH

Every word listed below is contained within this group of letters. Words can be found horizontally, vertically, or diagonally. They may read either backward or forward. The leftover letters reveal the end of a quote from the know-it-all droid C-3PO that begins: "Don't worry about Master Luke. I'm sure he's all right…"

```
Q I H U K O O D T N U O C
U A D O Y E M P I R E L D
E E S E C D Q I E U O O A
E J A R J A R B I N K S R
N I O A T E A O E C E N T
A F H T I S L N I W E A H
M N E S T V E E O D N H V
I O R H D A R K S I D E A
D G G T Y N S N O G O S D
A I U A K A N A O A R L E
L U K E S K Y W A L K E R
A Q L D W I F I O A R B A
N H U E M N A B N X B E E
D I E E I K O O W Y N R G
O J A B B A T H E H U T T
```

ANAKIN
CLONE
COUNT DOOKU
DARK SIDE
DARTH VADER
DEATH STAR
DROID
EMPIRE (The)
ENDOR
EWOKS
FORCE (The)
GALAXY
HAN SOLO
JABBA THE HUTT
JAR JAR BINKS
JEDI
LANDO
LEIA
LIGHTSABER
LUKE SKYWALKER
OBI-WAN KENOBI
QUEEN AMIDALA
QUI-GON
REBELS
SITH
WOOKIEE
YODA

Hidden quote: ______________________________

Answers on page 172.

L'adder

ANALYSIS COMPUTATION

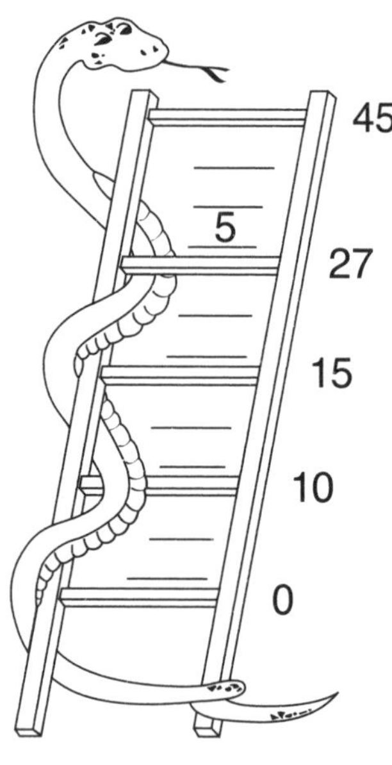

Starting at the bottom rung, use the numbers 1 through 9 to add up to the top number. Numbers can only be used once. There's a catch though: The precise sums must be met along the way.

A Puzzling Perspective

LANGUAGE SPATIAL VISUALIZATION

Mentally arrange the lettered balls from large to small in the correct order to spell an 11-letter word.

Clue: Pertaining to air

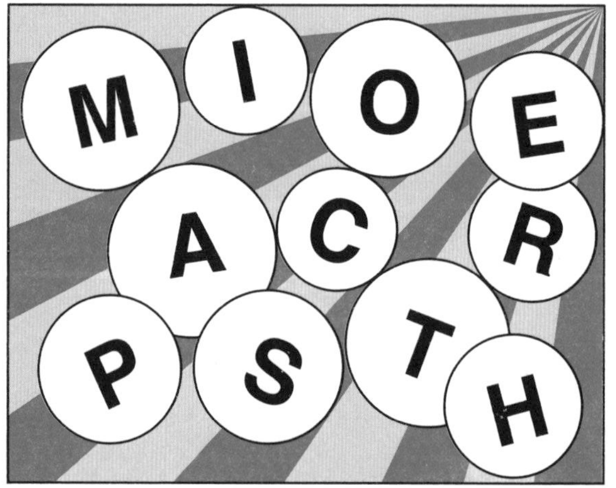

Answers on page 173.

Fitting Words

GENERAL KNOWLEDGE | PLANNING

In this miniature crossword, the clues are listed randomly and are numbered for convenience only. It is up to you to figure out the placement of the 9 answers. To help you, we've inserted one letter in the grid, and this is the only occurrence of that letter in the puzzle.

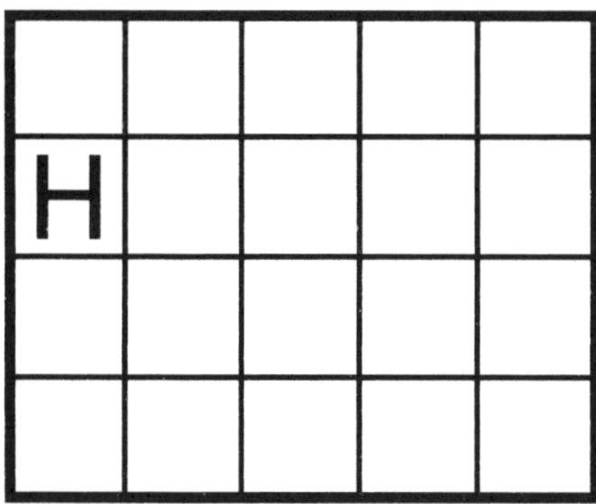

Clues

1. Stuck, as in mud
2. Antidote
3. Mattress part
4. Residence
5. 1981 Warren Beatty epic
6. Winter coasters
7. Preowned
8. Happen
9. Resistance units

Calcu-doku

COMPUTATION | LOGIC

Use arithmetic and deductive logic to complete the grid so that each row and column contains the numbers 1 through 4 in some order. Numbers in each outlined set of squares combine to produce the number in the top corner using the mathematical sign indicated. The solution is unique.

4×	8×	3	4+
		2	
9+		4×	
		6+	

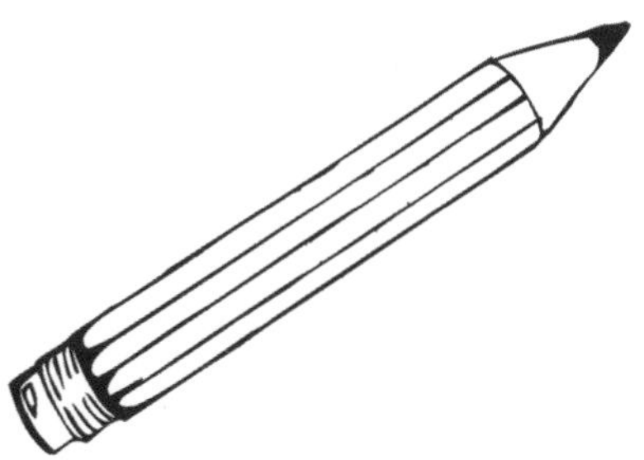

Answers on page 173.

Flip the Cards

ANALYSIS LOGIC

Three cards have been laid out, each marked with a letter on one side and a number on the other. If you want to make sure that every card with a 6 has a G on the other side, and that cards with an R have a 5 on the other side, which cards need to be turned over?

A. All 3 cards
B. The card on the left and the card on the right
C. The card on the right and the card in the middle
D. The card on the left and the card in the middle

Word Jigsaw

LANGUAGE PLANNING

Fit the pieces into the frame to form common words reading across and down. There's no need to rotate the pieces; they'll fit as shown, with each piece used once.

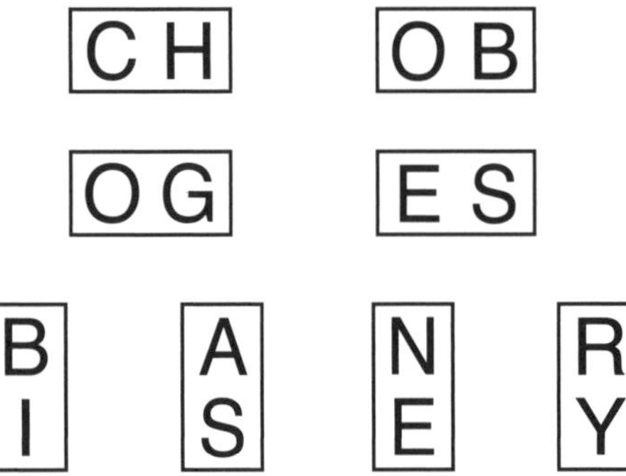

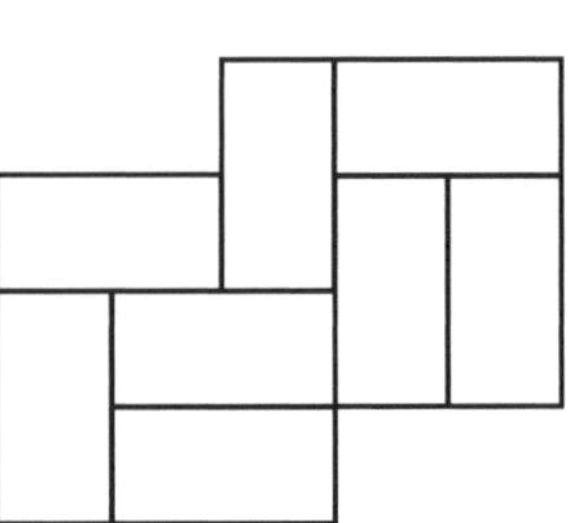

Answers on page 173.

Alien Mutations

PLANNING VISUAL LOGIC

Shown are 9 mutation chambers surrounded by alien figures. Each of the 3 aliens on the left passed through the 3 chambers to their right and transformed into the figure on the other side (e.g. the alien on the left of A passed through chambers A, B, and C and mutated into the alien to the right of C). The same is true for the aliens above the chambers: Each passed through the 3 chambers directly below them and came out mutated on the other side.

Each chamber affects 1—and only 1—alteration (changes in head or body shape, changes in posture, addition/removal of appendages). Note: Some chambers in the same row or column will undo what a previous chamber has done.

What mutation is each chamber responsible for?

Answers on page 173.

Seafood Dinner Date

GENERAL KNOWLEDGE | LANGUAGE

1	2	3	4	■	5	6	7	8	9	■	10	11	12	13
14				■	15					■	16			
17				18						■	19			
20			■	21				■	22	23				
24			25		■	26		27				■	■	■
■	■	■	28		29	■	■	30				31	32	33
34	35	36		■	37	38	39		■	40				
41				■	42				43	■	44			
45				46	■	47				■	48			
49					50		■	■	51	52		■	■	■
■	■	■	53				54	55	■	56		57	58	59
60	61	62				■	63		64		■	65		
66				■	67	68					69			
70				■	71					■	72			
73				■	74					■	75			

ACROSS

1. Major police announcements: abbr.
5. Li'l one in the comics
10. Shawl or stole
14. Soft, amorphous mass
15. Make happen
16. Golfer's target
17. "How would you describe your date's demeanor?"
19. Egyptian snakes
20. Geisha's sash
21. Fusses
22. Bear witness
24. Coral formations
26. Lipton competitor
28. Hallucination-inducing drug, initially
30. Photographer's cover
34. Not to mention
37. River to the Seine

40. Disgrace
41. Swain
42. Statement of belief
44. Icy coating
45. Comedian Bruce
47. Poker entrance fee
48. Privy to
49. Squeezed (out)
51. "Delicious!"
53. Exit
56. Separate
60. Symbol of limpness
63. Bangkok native
65. Water closet, in London
66. Jai _________
67. "Did you talk much?"
70. Bo's'n's boss
71. "_________ say more?"
72. Head of France?
73. Cassini of fashion
74. Lip application
75. Change for a five

DOWN

1. Despise
2. First-year West Pointer
3. Alamo defender Jim
4. Govt. org. for entrepreneurs
5. Part of USNA: abbr.
6. Breakfast sizzler
7. Hospital employee
8. Spanish "that"
9. Manufacturer's money-back offer
10. "I heard your date wasn't very tall?"
11. American Beauty, e.g.
12. Swiss mountain chain
13. Irksome one
18. Backtalk
23. Jacks take them
25. "What was your date's reaction when the check came?"
27. Winter weather forecast
29. "What's up, _________?"
31. A son of Adam
32. Bullets, briefly
33. Hammer end
34. Up to the task
35. Soup ingredient
36. In one's right mind
38. Hopping mad
39. D.C. bigwig
43. Rep.'s foe
46. Lotus position discipline
50. Egging on
52. Seriously injure
54. Canonized pope known as "the Great"
55. Herring family members
57. Mayflower Pilgrim John
58. Mail carrier's beat
59. Drinks to excess
60. Texas city on the Brazos
61. Israeli carrier
62. Gift-wrapping need
64. Author Kingsley
68. Disney cartoon collectible
69. DDE's WWII sphere

Answers on page 173.

Pampered Pups

ATTENTION VISUAL SEARCH

Find the 14 differences between these 2 doggy salon scenes.

Answers on page 173.

Vex-a-Gon

CREATIVE THINKING | PLANNING

Place the numbers 1 through 6 into the triangles of each hexagon. The numbers may be in any order, but they do not repeat within each hexagon shape.

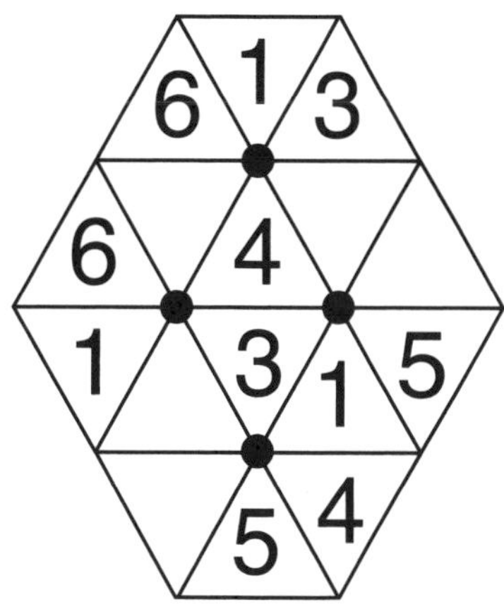

Name Calling

ANALYSIS

1	2 ABC	3 DEF
4 GHI	5 JKL	6 MNO
7 PQRS	8 TUV	9 WXYZ
	0	

Decipher the encoded words in the saying below using the numbers and letters on the phone pad. Remember that each number can stand for 3 or 4 possible letters.

One 4–6–6–3 deed has many 2–5–2–4–6–2–6–8–7.

Answers on page 173.

Clapboard

GENERAL KNOWLEDGE | LANGUAGE

Like a crossword puzzle, the goal here is to find the word or words best suited for the given clues. But unlike a crossword, there are no boxes that separate one word from another. In fact, words on the same line often blend together. The letters at the end of one word sometimes form the beginning of the next, but only on the same line; words never carry over from one row or column to the next.

1	2	3	4	5	6	7	8	9	10	11	12	13
14				15				16				
17					18			19	20	21		
22	23		24		25		26		27		28	
29				30		31	32	33		34		35
36	37	38	39				40			41		
42			43		44	45	46	47				48
49			50				51			52		
53	54	55	56	57			58		59			
60		61			62			63		64	65	66
67	68		69	70		71	72		73			
74				75				76		77		
78			79		80				81			

ACROSS

1. He cuts hair
6. TV control
11. Flow out
14. Ward off
15. Seer's card
16. Striped predator
17. Get back
18. It's presented at a trial
20. Cry on the links
22. Forehead
24. More sage
26. Disprove

29. Showers
30. Soft drink
32. War god
34. Instant lawn material
36. Leer
39. George who was Mary
40. Camper's need
41. Play about Capote
42. Dry
43. River's mouth, sometimes
46. Doing sums
49. Take the plunge
50. Fencers' foils
51. Ooze
52. Bogey beater
53. Copy
55. Tolkien tree creature
57. More edgy
59. Commuted
60. Mexicali misters
62. Fly high
63. Spoil
64. Foot digit
67. Bedazzled
69. Motor city
73. Spill the beans
74. Second-place finisher
75. KC pro
76. "Salem's ________"
77. Golf ball holder
78. Little ones
79. It comes from trees
80. He sang about a magic dragon
81. Crucifix

DOWN

1. Cutting comment
2. Declare
3. Flinch
4. Toasted
5. Needle cases
6. Makes music?
7. Went the wrong way
8. Anchor
9. Oklahoma native
10. Spat
11. Conceit
12. Ernie's pal
13. Lineage
19. Poetic contraction
21. Throw out
22. Wide
23. Tatter
25. Get dirty
26. Squealer
27. Bends in a crash
28. Transport to Oz
30. Took a nap
31. Period
33. Embarrassed
35. Made a hole
37. Hold on tightly
38. Pep up
39. Idyllic place
40. Former Soviet news agency
41. Gratuity
43. Lair
44. Dregs
45. Choir part
47. Bucks, e.g.
48. From Athens
49. German article
52. Sort of soup
54. Sunday seat
56. Protuberances
57. Uno y dos
58. ________ Paulo
59. Helicopter part
60. Ice melter
61. Brooding place
62. Sort of sign
63. Vex
65. Butter substitute
66. Supplemented with difficulty
68. Court
70. Time to remember
71. Bread choice
72. Trigger treat

Answers on page 174.

Clone It!

CREATIVE THINKING | SPATIAL VISUALIZATION | VISUAL LOGIC

Use the grid dots as a guide to separate the shaded shape into 2 smaller shapes that are either identical or mirror each other.

For a hint, study this example illustration:

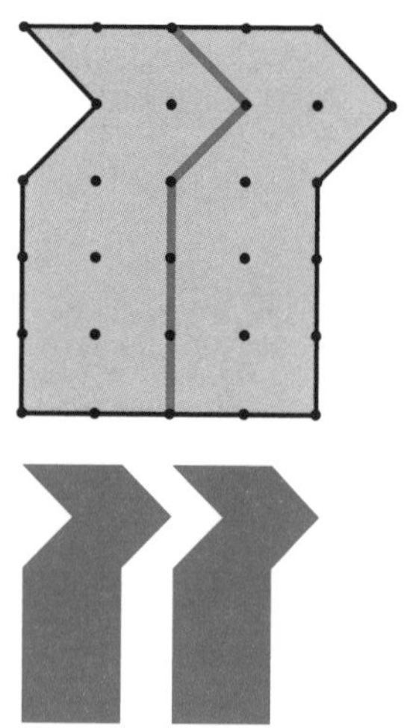

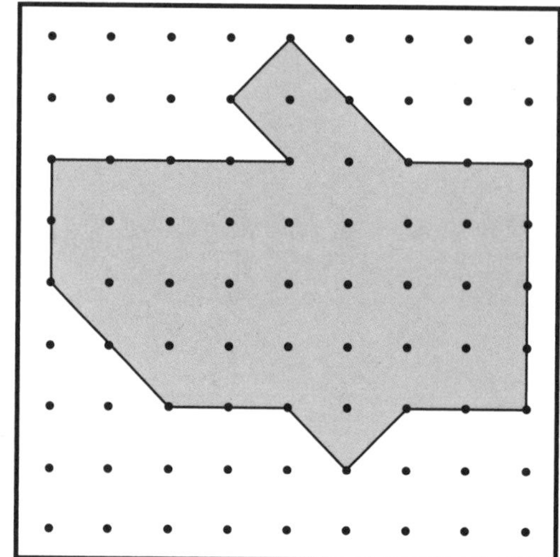

Cast-a-Word

LOGIC | PROBLEM SOLVING

There are 4 dice, and there are different letters of the alphabet on the 6 faces of each of them (each letter appears only once). Random throws of the dice produced the words in this list. Can you figure out which letters appear on each of the 4 dice?

BARD	FORD	JILT	PECK	SODA
BRIG	GLOW	LAZY	QUIP	STAG
DAUB	HOLE	NAME	SEAM	YOLK

Answers on page 174.

Team Search

ATTENTION VISUAL SEARCH

Every team listed below is contained within this group of letters. Teams can be found in a straight line horizontally, vertically, or diagonally. They may be read either backward or forward. Leftover letters reveal a quote from Mickey Mantle.

Bonus: What team is missing from this list?

```
A T E A M S S I S S W H E B R
E S A B B T S C R A N G E R S
O E S Y R N S E I K C O R E N
C E A R I A G Y N T N P R W A
O K V L E I V A A E E H I E I
S N R C T G T E O J U L P R D
R A S A S I D S S T E M H S N
M Y E A O L G O N E O U I T I
N S T N H C A R D I N A L S A
I E A G A S O Y W N W S L B A
G L R E D S O X O S E T I H W
S O I L A N T M A R I N E R S
G I P S I S W R D A E H S E B
R R E A C O W A O Y A D R D U
G O O E S T P O H S I D S E C
```

ANGELS	BREWERS	INDIANS	ORIOLES	RAYS	TIGERS
ASTROS	CARDINALS	MARINERS	PADRES	REDS	TWINS
ATHLETICS	CUBS	MARLINS	PHILLIES	RED SOX	WHITE SOX
BLUE JAYS	DODGERS	METS	PIRATES	ROCKIES	YANKEES
BRAVES	GIANTS	NATIONALS	RANGERS	ROYALS	

Hidden quote: ____

Answers on page 174.

Perfect Score

COMPUTATION VISUAL LOGIC

Make 3 successful hits so that the sum of the numbers is 100. Double and triple scores do not apply. Numbers may be used more than once.

Crypto-Group: Comic Book Heroes

LANGUAGE LOGIC

Cryptograms are messages in substitution code. Break the code to reveal the 5 comic-book heroes. For example, THE SMART CAT might become FVO QWGDF JGF if **F** is substituted for **T, V** for **H, O** for **E,** and so on.

S L B X L V

R L K P R P Y N T

S T L O A F N R M F

N K M V C N I B

O J O T M H I

Answers on page 174.

Level 2

Quic-Kross

GENERAL KNOWLEDGE | LANGUAGE

This is a crossword puzzle with a twist. Use the clues to solve the puzzle. When complete, the circled letters will spell out a "mystery word."

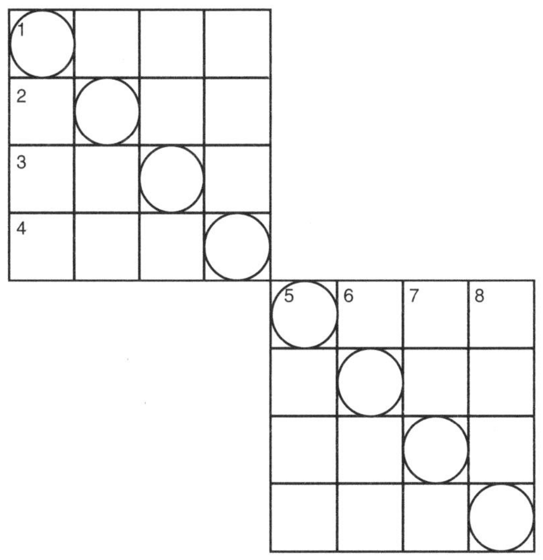

ACROSS

1. Floating craft
2. Metric weight measure
3. Thermal energy
4. Suspend

DOWN

5. Small, rough particle
6. Silicon oxide granule
7. Market place
8. Small pie

Mystery word clue: Boaster

Word Ladder

LANGUAGE | PLANNING

Use the clues to change just one letter on each line to go from the top word to the bottom word. Do not change the order of the letters. You must have a common English word at each step.

GRATE

_____ angry

_____ you can pack it full and transport goods within it

_____ a metal structure used for lifting and moving things

_____ wicked-looking elderly woman

DRONE

Answers on page 174.

Naughty Students

LOGIC

Four students are in front of the principal for breaking rules. The principal's secretary has made a list of the crimes and designated punishment for each student, but she has mixed up the details. Although each item is in the correct column, only 1 item in each column is correctly positioned. The following facts are true about the correct order:

1. Goof is 1 place below Colin and 2 places below stealing books.
2. Forfeiting sport is 2 places above talking back.
3. Cleaning windows is 1 place below Finkel and 1 place above Denzil.

Can you give the correct name, surname, crime, and punishment for each position?

	Name	Surname	Crime	Punishment
1	Andy	Everong	eating in class	cleaning windows
2	Bernard	Finkel	breaking chairs	mopping floors
3	Colin	Goof	talking back	forfeiting sport
4	Denzil	Harrow	stealing books	extra assignments

Trivia on the Brain

When fighting with yourself, most people imagine a devil on one shoulder and an angel on the other. Turns out that's not far from the truth. The part of you that thinks, "Why I ought to—!" and imagines deliciously aggressive thoughts is your amygdala, and the part that says, "Maybe that isn't so wise," is your prefrontal cortex. How can you help your angel win the war? Take a long breath before action to give it time to restrain your emotional response.

Answer on page 174.

ABCD

LOGIC PLANNING

A	2	1	1	3	0	2
B	1	3	2	0	1	2
C	2	1	2	1	3	0
D	1	1	1	2	2	2

A	B	C	D						
2	2	2	0						
1	3	0	2						
2	1	1	2						
0	2	2	2						
3	1	1	1						
1	0	3	2						

Every cell in this grid contains 1 of 4 letters: A, B, C, or D. No letter can be horizontally or vertically adjacent to itself. The tables above and to the left of the grid indicate how many times each letter appears in that column or row. Can you complete the grid?

Calcu-doku

COMPUTATION LOGIC

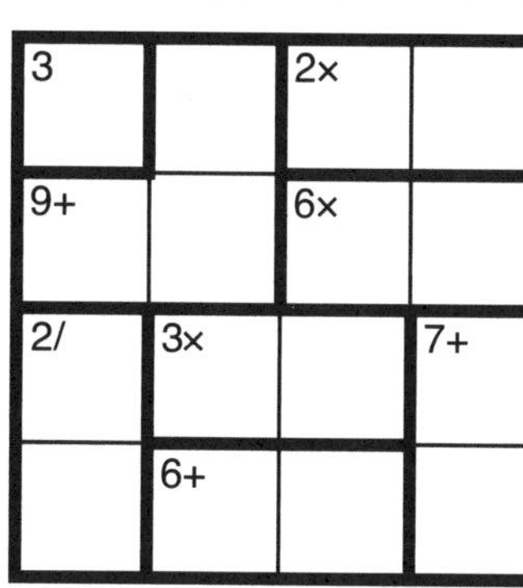

Use arithmetic and deductive logic to complete the grid so that each row and column contains the numbers 1 through 4 in some order. Numbers in each outlined set of squares combine to produce the number in the top corner using the mathematical sign indicated. The solution is unique.

Answers on page 174.

Elevator Words

GENERAL KNOWLEDGE | LANGUAGE

Like an elevator, words move up and down the "floors" of this puzzle. Starting with the first answer, the second word from each answer carries down to become the first word of the following answer. With the clues given, complete the puzzle.

1. Expertise	1. Know _______
2. "Why?"	2. _______ _______
3. Confess	3. _______ _______
4. Innocence	4. _______ _______
5. "Don't Touch!"	5. _______ _______
6. Mistaken	6. _______ _______
7. Single, in baseball	7. _______ Hit

Fences

ANALYSIS | LOGIC

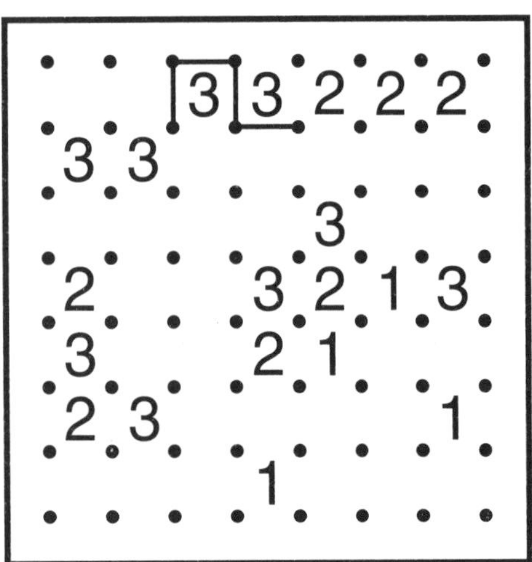

Connect the dots and draw a continuous path that doesn't cross itself. Numbers represent the "fences" created by the path (2 edges are created around the number 2, 3 edges around 3, etc.). We've started the puzzle for you.

Answers on pages 174–175.

What's Flipped in Vegas, Stays in Vegas

COMPUTATION | PROBLEM SOLVING

Vivian loved Las Vegas. After seeing all the hottest shows, eating at all the hottest buffets, and walking down the hottest strip, Vivian was ready to try some gambling. Unfortunately, the only game she knew was flipping coins. Luckily, she found Caesar's Shack, a tiny casino that catered to coin-flippers. The croupier—or in this case, flippier—invited her to play the house game. He would let her flip a coin 20 times. Each time the coin landed on heads, he would pay her $2. Each time the coin landed on tails, she had to pay him $3. Vivian was on edge but decided to give it a try. She flipped the coin 20 times and left Caesar's Shack with the same amount of money she came in with. How many times did the coin come up heads?

Sudoku

LOGIC

					1			5
		6	2		4		7	
	4	7		3				
		4				7	3	
	7		3	8	2		9	
	8	3				6		
				9		8	2	
	5		1		8	3		
3			7					

Use deductive logic to complete the grid so that each row, each column, and each 3 by 3 box contains the numbers 1 through 9 in some order. The solution is unique.

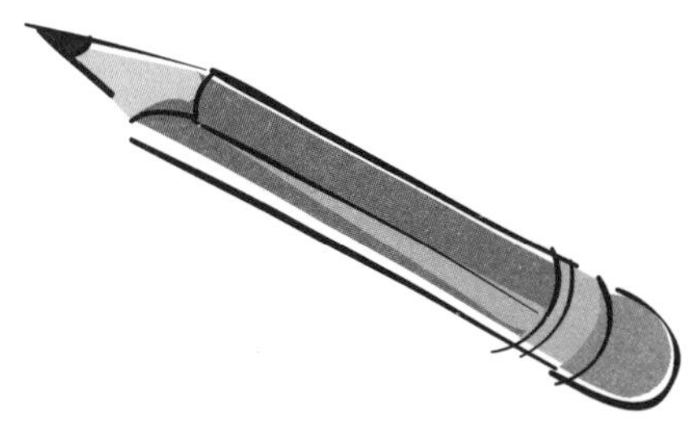

Answers on page 175.

Spell Math!

ANALYSIS COMPUTATION

Spell out numbers in the blanks below to obtain the correct solution. Numbers are used only once and range from 1 to 20. A letter has been given to get you started.

S ___ ___ + ___ ___ ___ ___ = ___ ___ ___ ___ ___ ___ ___

Fit It

ANALYSIS PLANNING

Use each of the names found in the list below to complete the clue-less crossword grid on the next page. The puzzle has only one solution.

4 letters
Gena
Lena
Lola
Nora
Oona
Skye

5 letters
Diana
Gilda
Peggy
Teena

6 letters
Angela
Zsa Zsa

7 letters
Lucy Liu
Meg Ryan
Wynonna

8 letters
Ann Curry

9 letters
Demi Moore
Etta Place
Kelly Ripa

10 letters
Jill St. John
Sophia Bush

11 letters
Ellen Pompeo
Hilary Swank
Katie Couric
Marsha Mason
Rachel Weisz
Sharon Stone
Teri Hatcher

12 letters
Kate Bosworth
Kristin Davis
Nicole Kidman
Toni Collette

13 letters
Heather Graham
Jennifer Lopez

14 letters
Jamie Lee Curtis

15 letters
Evangeline Lilly
Mariska Hargitay

16 letters
Jada Pinkett Smith

17 letters
Scarlett Johansson

18 letters
Sarah Jessica Parker

Answer on page 175.

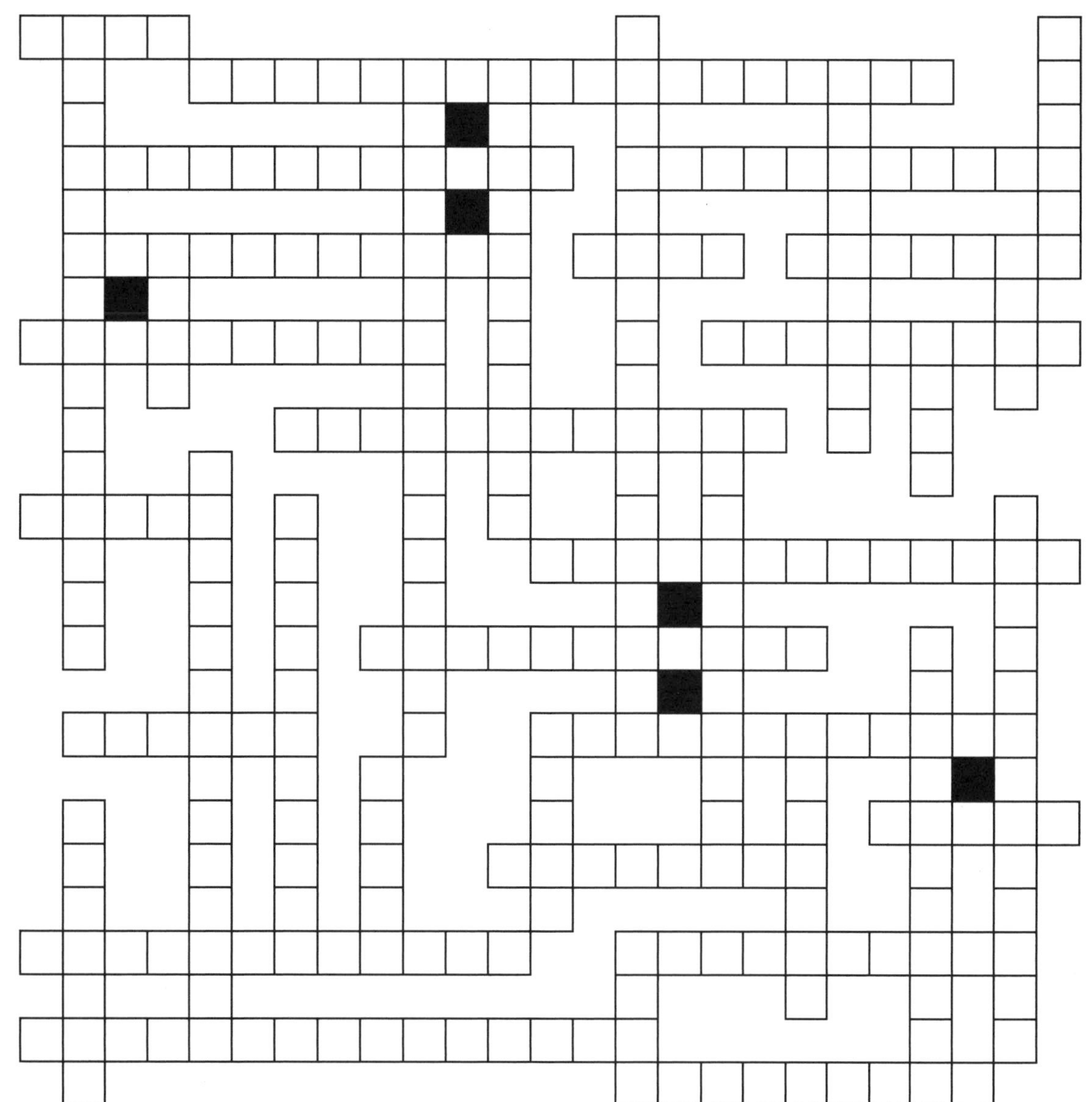

Trivia on the Brain

It takes only 10 seconds for someone to lose consciousness once blood flow is blocked from the brain.

Answer on page 175.

Retro Rocket Maze

PLANNING

SPATIAL REASONING

Get ready to blast off as you work your way through this puzzle!

Answer on page 175.

Word-a-Maze: Measured

CREATIVE THINKING | GENERAL KNOWLEDGE

Travel in sequence through the puzzle from the left side to the right, using each numbered clue to determine the correct word. Connect adjacent words with a common letter to proceed through the maze. Some letters are already given. The first and last words tie into the title.

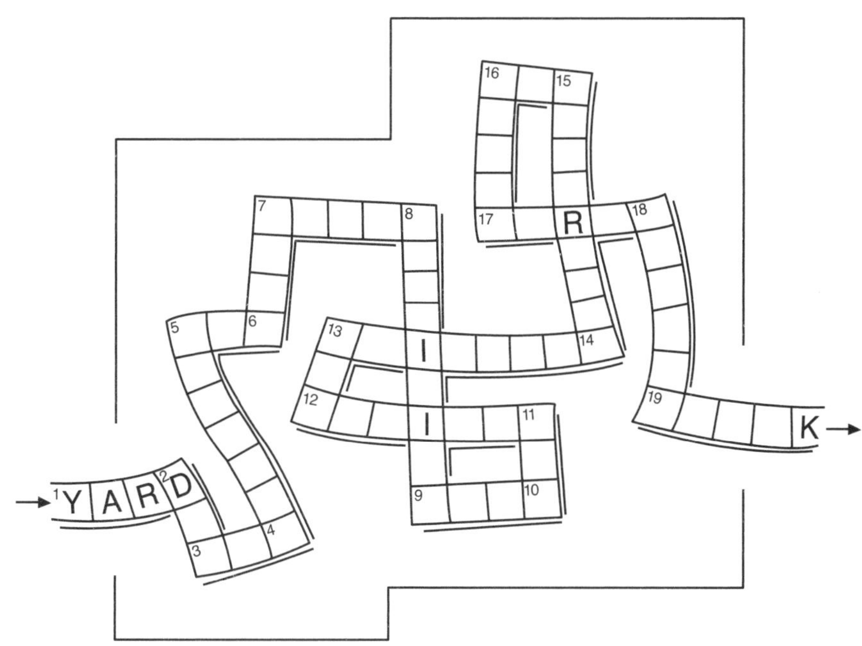

1. Lawn
2. Headlight setting
3. Scar
4. Saved
5. Batman and Robin
6. Smell
7. Not left
8. Frightens
9. Musical offering
10. Fastball, slang
11. Hypodermic needle
12. Will Ferrell movie
13. Dessert
14. Moves to another country
15. Drunk
16. Part of a bride's gown
17. Up direction
18. Hoofed animals
19. Twig

Answers on page 175.

Star Power

LOGIC PLANNING

Fill in each square in the grid so that each star is surrounded by the numbers 1 through 8 with no repeats.

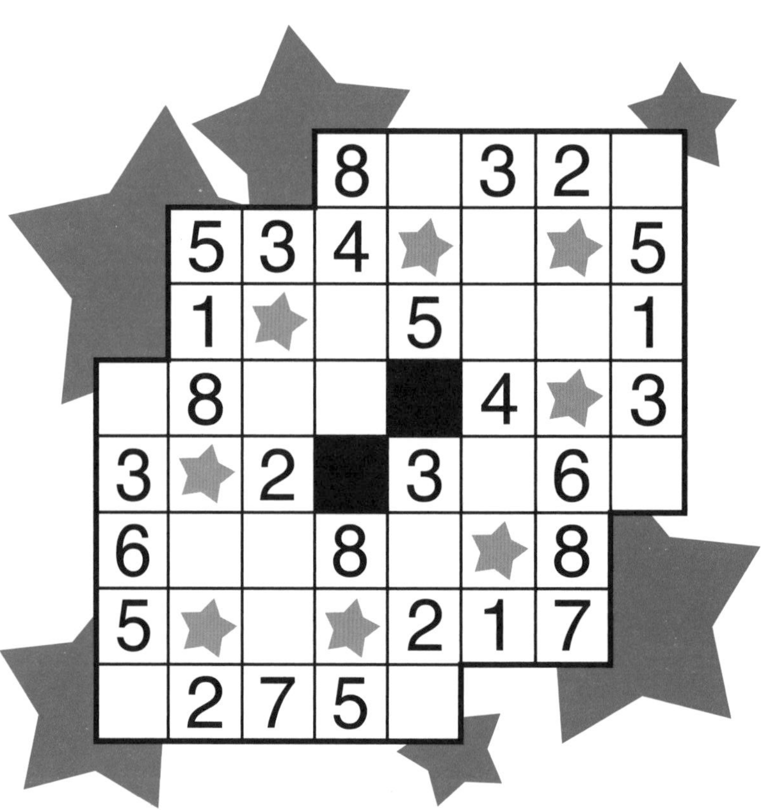

Trivia on the Brain

Are you sluggish in the morning? Start your day right by rehydrating your body. You've just spent a third of your day without drinking anything, and your brain needs water to function. It also needs blood, so get your heart pumping by doing a few jumping jacks.

Answer on page 175.

1-2-3

LOGIC **PLANNING**

Place the numbers 1, 2, and 3 in the circles below. The challenge is to have only these 3 numbers in each connected row and column—no number should repeat. Any combination is allowed.

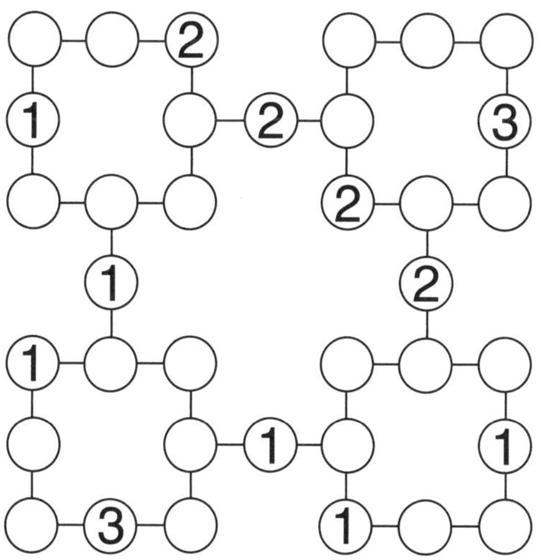

Word Ladder

LANGUAGE **PLANNING**

Use the clues to change just one letter on each line to go from the top word to the bottom word. Do not change the order of the letters. You must have a common English word at each step.

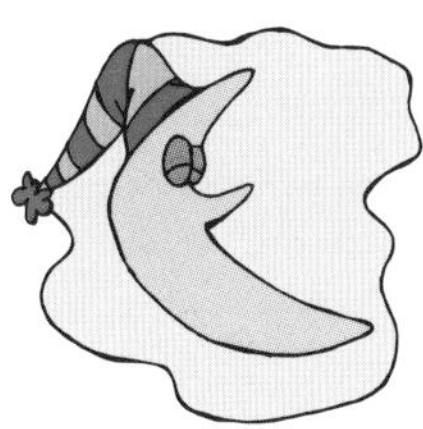

SLEEP

______ icy rain

______ took a nap

______ used a broom

______ not bitter

SKEET

Answers on page 176.

Word Columns

LANGUAGE PLANNING

Find the quote from Napolean Bonaparte by using the letters directly above each of the blank squares. Each letter is used only once. A black square indicates the end of a word.

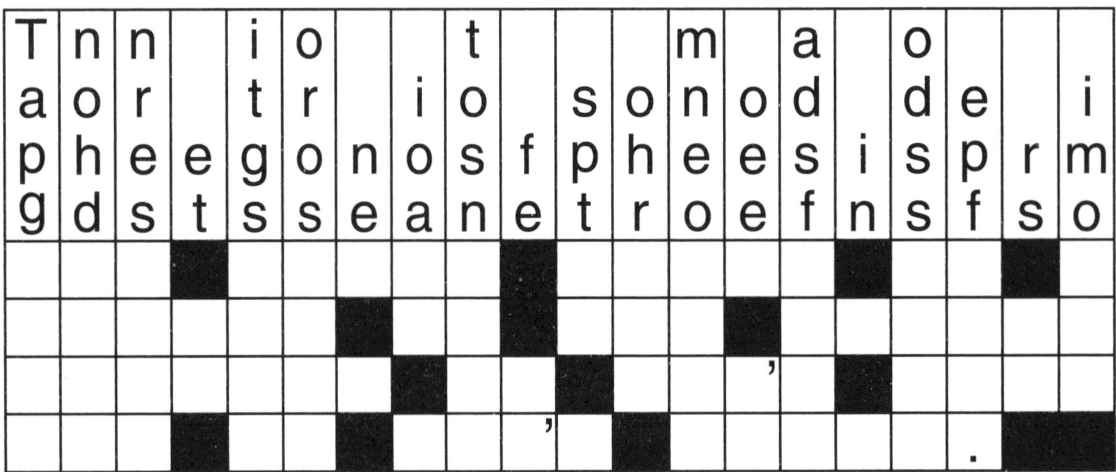

T	n	n		i	o			t				m		a		o			
a	o	r		t	r		i	o		s	o	n	o	d		d	e		i
p	h	e	e	g	o	n	o	s	f	p	h	e	e	s	i	s	p	r	m
g	d	s	t	s	s	e	a	n	e	t	r	o	e	f	n	s	f	s	o
			■						■						■			■	
						■			■				■						
							■			■			’		■				
			■			■			’		■						.	■	■

Minesweeper

ANALYSIS LOGIC

There are 20 hidden mines in the grid. Numbers indicate the amount of mines adjacent to that square horizontally, vertically, and diagonally. We entered the first 1 to get you started.

3			1			1			1	✹✹
		2			1		1			✹✹
3				2					1	✹✹
1		2	1			1				✹✹
						1	1	✹		✹✹
		1		1				2		✹✹
			1	1		1		1	1	✹✹
2			2							✹✹
		1				1				✹✹
1			1		2	1			3	✹

Answers on page 176.

Cross Count

COMPUTATION LANGUAGE

All the letters of the alphabet have been assigned a value from 1 through 9, as demonstrated in the box below. Fill in the grid with common English words so that the rows and columns add up correctly.

1	2	3	4	5	6	7	8	9
a	b	c	d	e	f	g	h	i
j	k	l	m	n	o	p	q	r
s	t	u	v	w	x	y	z	

7 p	1	9 r	17
		1	15
			12
14	15	15	

Double Jumble

LANGUAGE

It's 2 jumbles in 1! First, unscramble the 7 letters under each row of squares to form common English words. When you've done this, unscramble the letters running down each column in the dark boxes to reveal 2 more words.

M I A D L M E

N I R T M I A

G L A T E E N

G C O A T N O

H R A L T E E

Answers on page 176.

GET YOUR NOODLE COOKING

LEVEL 3

Animal House?

LANGUAGE LOGIC

Cryptograms are messages in substitution code. Break the code to read the humorous quote and its speaker. For example, THE SMART CAT might become FVO QWGDF JGF if **F** is substituted for **T, V** for **H, O** for **E,** and so on.

"K DGNVKWGS K PNX STXVGUKI PFGJ K PGJZ ZQ N ZQBN ANDZT SDGXXGS NX N BQNZ."

—IQCGSKNJ CNDIYX HDKBXZQIRG

Kakuro

ANALYSIS COMPUTATION

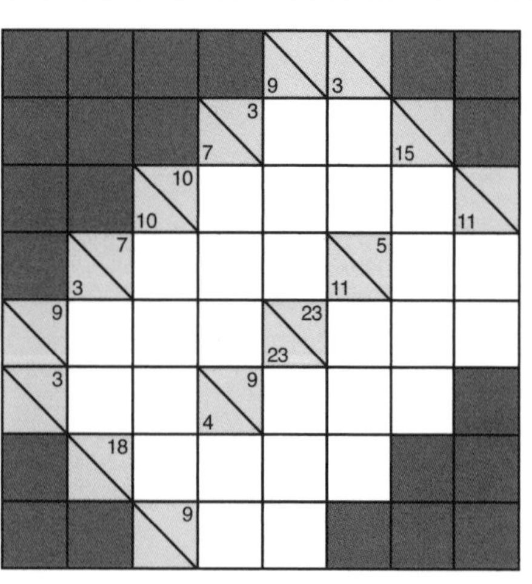

Place a number from 1 through 9 in each empty cell so that the sum of each vertical or horizontal run (rows and columns extending from already numbered cells) equals the number at the top or on the left of that run. Numbers may not be repeated in any run, and runs end at dark-colored squares.

Answers on page 176.

Hitori

PLANNING VISUAL LOGIC

The object of this puzzle is to have a number appear only once in each row and column. By shading a number cell, you are effectively removing that number from its row and column. There's a catch though: Shaded number cells are never adjacent to one another in a row or column.

1	5	3	5	8	1	2	8
2	5	8	3	5	6	1	4
5	5	4	7	6	1	8	2
6	7	5	1	3	3	3	8
3	8	2	6	1	5	4	4
4	5	6	1	3	3	5	7
2	4	1	2	5	7	1	6
8	1	7	3	2	5	6	3

Spell Math!

ANALYSIS COMPUTATION

Spell out numbers in the blanks below to obtain the correct solution. Numbers are used only once and range from 1 to 20. A letter has been given to get you started.

___ ___ ___ ___ + ___ ___ ___ ___ = t ___ ___ ___ ___ ___ ___ ___

Answers on page 176.

Missing Connections

LANGUAGE PLANNING

It's a crossword without the clues! Use the letters below to fill in the empty spaces in the crossword grid. When you are finished, you'll have words that read both across and down, crossword-style.

A A A A A C D E E E E I I F L L L

N N P R R S S T T W Y Y

Word Jigsaw

LANGUAGE PLANNING

Fit the pieces into the frame to form common words reading across and down. There's no need to rotate the pieces; they'll fit as shown, with each piece used once.

PE AS

RI LK

H/A H/E C/E E/G

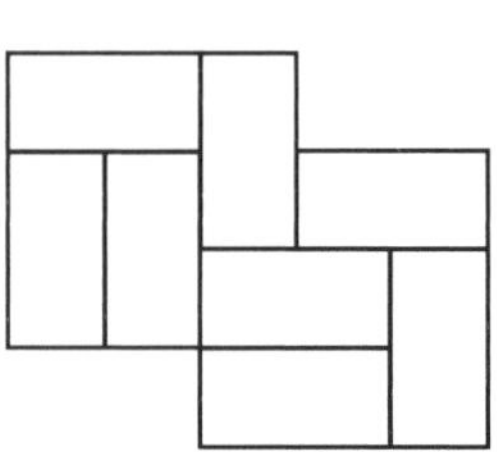

Answers on page 176.

CREATIVE THINKING

SPATIAL VISUALIZATION

VISUAL LOGIC

Uncrossed Paths

Draw lines to like symbols (triangle to triangle, star to star) without any line crossing another line.

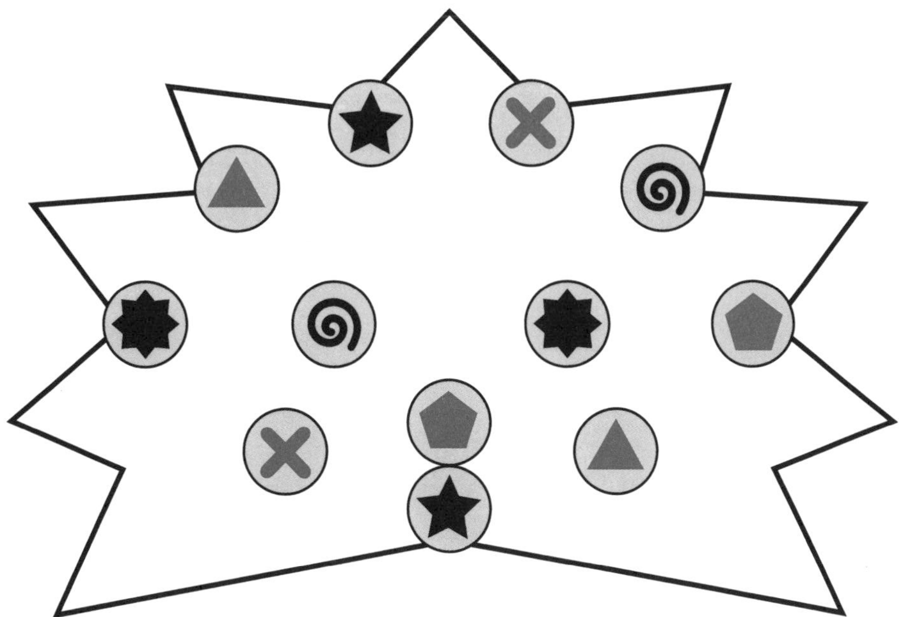

Trivia on the Brain

Just like some people need a harder physical workout than others, some need a more vigorous mental workout, too. So, in addition to working these puzzles, try brushing your teeth or eating a bowl of cereal using the opposite hand. Or take up a new hobby that puts fine-motor skills to work, such as painting, sewing, or playing an instrument.

Answer on page 177.

Sudoku

LOGIC

Use deductive logic to complete the grid so that each row, each column, and each 3 by 3 box contains the numbers 1 through 9 in some order. The solution is unique.

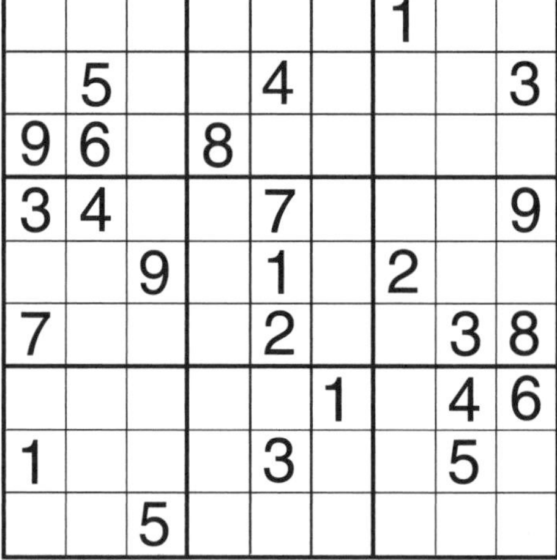

						1		
	5			4				3
9	6		8					
3	4			7				9
		9		1		2		
7				2			3	8
					1		4	6
1				3			5	
		5						

Eavesdropping Logic

ANALYSIS LOGIC

You overhear the following comment about a situation among some friends:

"When they heard the news, Belinda, Carl, and Simon reacted similarly, but one could see that Belinda alone was still considering her options. Simon and Carl seemed to realize there was nothing to be done."

From this passage, what can we gather?

A. That Belinda is more positive than the others.

B. That Belinda is lonelier than the others.

C. That Belinda is less fatalistic than the others.

D. There is not one sole option of the 3 above that fits.

Answers on page 177.

Elevator Words

GENERAL KNOWLEDGE | LANGUAGE

Like an elevator, words move up and down the "floors" of this puzzle. Starting with the first answer, the second word from each answer carries down to become the first word of the following answer. With the clues given, complete the puzzle.

1. Lump in the throat — 1. Adam's ______
2. Fruit source — 2. ______ ______
3. Bird bane — 3. ______ ______
4. Quack remedy — 4. ______ ______
5. Ecological nightmare — 5. ______ ______
6. Channel to carry off excess water — 6. ______ ______
7. A congratulation for solving this puzzle — 7. ______ to go

Vex-a-Gon

CREATIVE THINKING | PLANNING

Place the numbers 1 through 6 into the triangles of each hexagon. The numbers may be in any order, but they do not repeat within each hexagon shape.

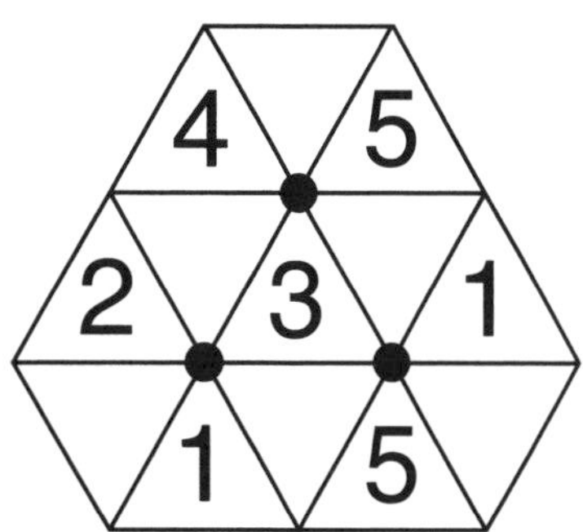

Answers on page 177.

Scientific Discoveries

LOGIC

In *Clock* magazine, the top 5 scientists in history have been listed with their discoveries. However, the items have been inadvertently mixed up. Although each item is in the correct column, only 1 item in each column is correctly positioned. The following facts are true about the correct order:

1. Eyeline is 2 places below eccentricity.
2. Newtune is not in first place.
3. Michael is 2 places above Bore.
4. Splitting apple is 2 places above Albert.
5. Niels is 3 places below gravy tree.

	Name	Surname	Discovery
1	Michael	Friday	eccentricity
2	Isaac	Newtune	gravy tree
3	Charles	Darling	devolution
4	Niels	Bore	splitting apple
5	Albert	Eyeline	relative pity

Can you find name, surname, and discovery for each position?

Mastermind

LOGIC

3	1	9	○
5	2	4	●
6	8	3	○
9	6	7	●
2	9	1	○
?	?	?	

Determine the correct order of the numbers at left with the help of the indicators given in each row. A black dot means that a number is in the correct position in that row; a white dot means the correct number is in that row, but in the wrong position. Digits do not appear more than once in the solution, and the solution never begins with 0.

Answers on page 177.

Diamond Mining

ATTENTION | VISUAL SEARCH

This diamond-shape grid contains 16 words and phrases that can precede or follow the word "diamond." The words can be found in a straight line horizontally, vertically, or diagonally. They may be read either forward or backward. When you have found all the words, the remaining letters spell a quote attributed to Confucius.

BACK

BASEBALL

DUST

HEAD

HOPE

IN THE ROUGH

JIM BRADY

JUBILEE

LEGS

LIL

MINE

NECKLACE

NEIL

RING

STATE

WEDDING

Hidden quote: ______________________________

Answers on page 177.

Grid Fill

LANGUAGE PLANNING

To complete this puzzle, place the given letters and words into the shapes on this grid. Words and letters will run across, down, and wrap around each shape. When the grid is filled, each row will contain one of the following words: drove, fable, hazel, rusty, tried, vices.

1. V

3. FAT, HAD

4. RICE, ZERO

5. BLEED, STYLE, VIRUS

Rhyme Time

GENERAL KNOWLEDGE LANGUAGE

Each clue leads to a 2-word answer that rhymes, such as BIG PIG or STABLE TABLE. The numbers in parentheses after the clue give the number of letters in each word. For example, "cookware taken from the oven (3, 3)" would be "hot pot."

1. Sagacious fellows (4, 4): ______________

2. Grassy city area with no illumination (4, 4): ______________

3. Having soreness while gathering fallen leaves (6, 6): ______________

4. Justification for a turncoat's crime (7, 6): ______________

5. Jacob's biblical twin's teeter-totters (5, 7): ______________

Answers on page 177.

Star Power

LOGIC **PLANNING**

Fill in each empty square so that each star is surrounded by the numbers 1 through 8 with no repeats.

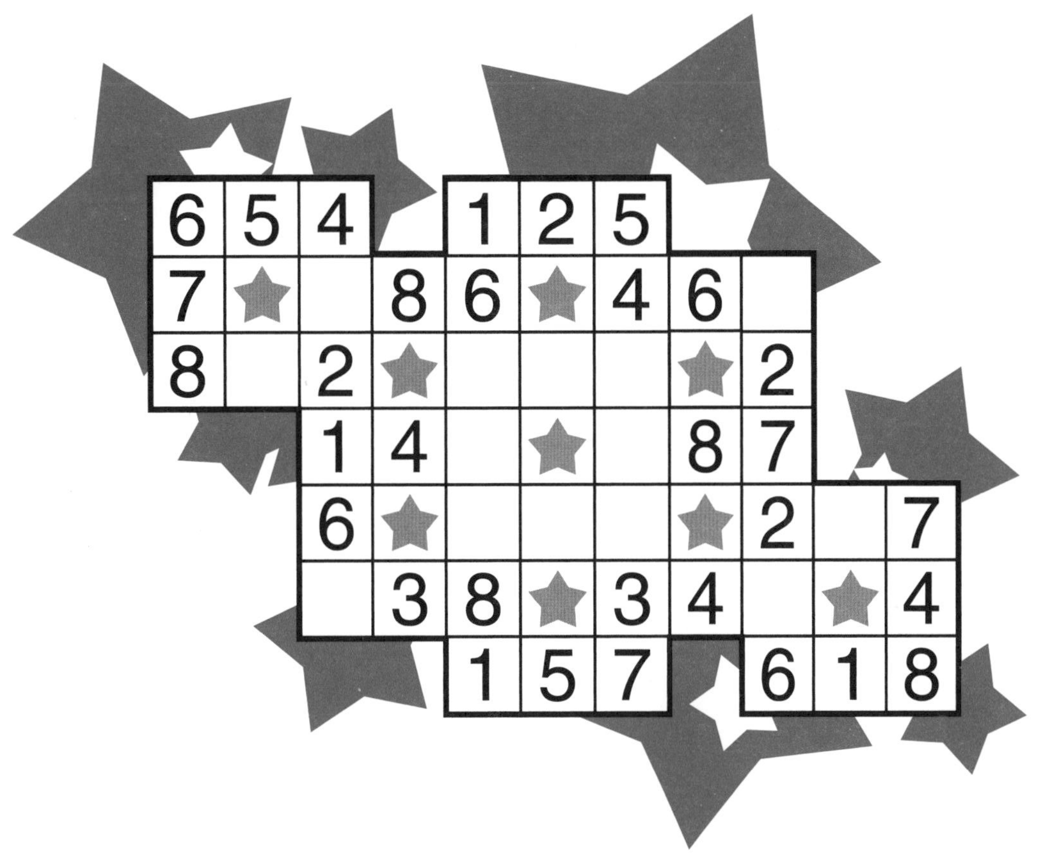

Trivia on the Brain

Of all the creatures on the earth, humans have the most complex brain.

Answer on page 177.

Anagram Snack

LANGUAGE

What 2 words, formed from different arrangements of the same 8 letters, can be used to complete the sentence below?

At the London teashop, you can use a prism to see an entire __________ of colors as you sip from your cup and munch on your __________.

Odd-Even Logidoku

LOGIC **PLANNING**

3	E	7		E	E			E
E					E		6	E
8		E			E	5	E	
		E	E		E	E		
	E	E		E		E		
	4			E			2	E
E	E		E					E
E			E			E	E	
		E	E	E		E		9

The numbers 1 through 9 are to appear once in every row, column, long diagonal, irregular shape, and 3 by 3 grid. Cells marked with the letter **E** contain even numbers. From the numbers given, can you complete the puzzle?

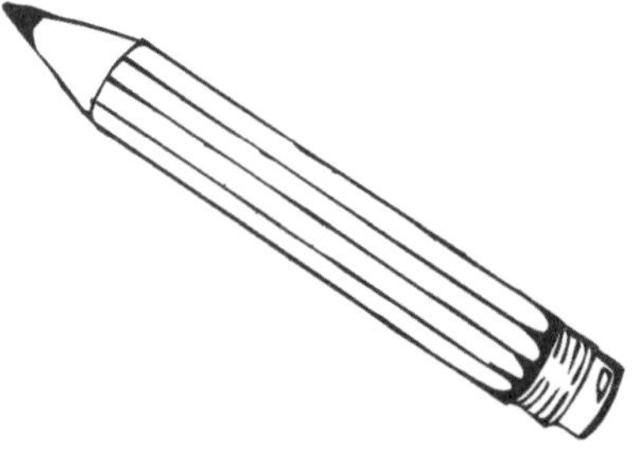

Answers on pages 177–178.

Discovering America by Alpha Sleuth™

LANGUAGE PLANNING

Move each of the letters below into the grid to form common words. You will use each letter once. The letters in the numbered cells of the grid correspond to the letters in the phrase at the bottom. Completing the grid will help you complete the phrase and vice versa. When finished, the grid and phrase will be filled with valid words, and you will have used all the letters in the letter set.

Hint: The numbered cells in the grid are arranged alphabetically, so the letter in the cell marked 1 will appear in the alphabet before the letter in the cell marked 2, and so on.

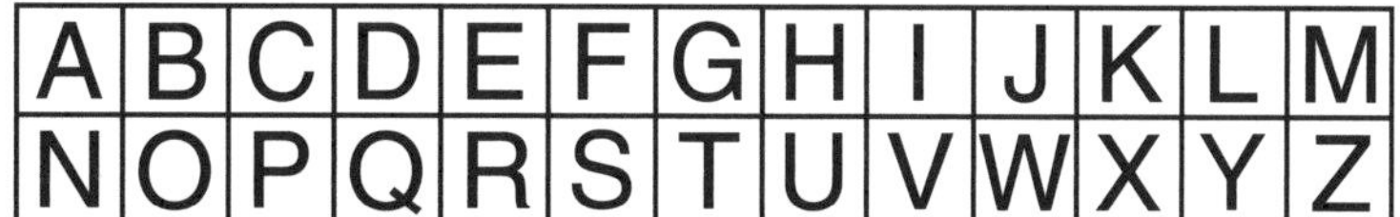

A	B	C	D	E	F	G	H	I	J	K	L	M
N	O	P	Q	R	S	T	U	V	W	X	Y	Z

Answer on page 178.

Calcu-doku

COMPUTATION LOGIC

Use arithmetic and deductive logic to complete the grid so that each row and column contains the numbers 1 through 5 in some order. Numbers in each outlined set of squares combine to produce the number in the top corner using the mathematical sign indicated. The solution is unique.

1	15×		2/	20×
9+	4+	40×		
				4+
	8×	6×		
5		1	6×	

Fitting Words

GENERAL KNOWLEDGE PLANNING

In this miniature crossword, the clues are listed randomly and are numbered for convenience only. It is up to you to figure out the placement of the 9 answers. To help you we've inserted one letter in the grid, and this is the only occurrence of that letter in the puzzle.

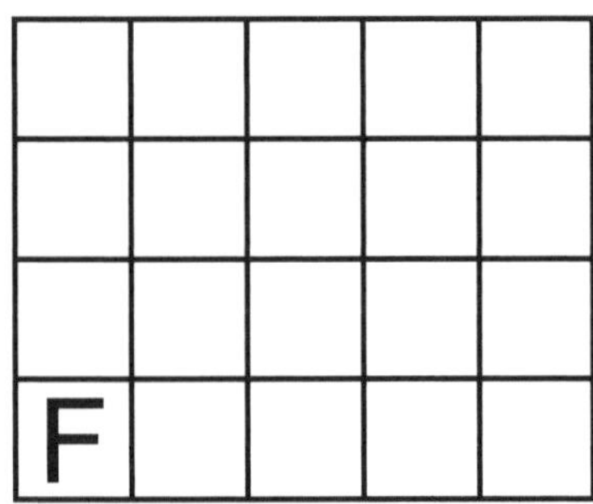

Clues

1. Latest thing
2. Let's go
3. Cognizant
4. Washstand jug
5. Spreadable cheese
6. Tarragon and thyme
7. Two quarters
8. Tennis divisions
9. Kosher

Answers on page 178.

Battle Boats

ANALYSIS LOGIC

Place each ship in the fleet located at right within the grid. Ships may be placed horizontally or vertically, but they don't touch each other, not even diagonally. Numbers reveal the ship segments located in that row or column.

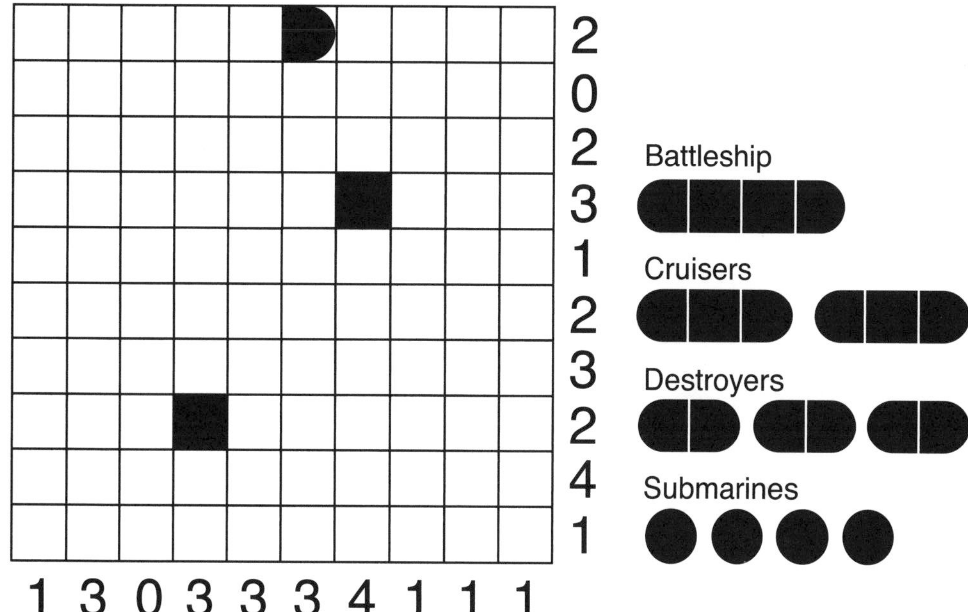

Trivia on the Brain

A study from 2003 found that 18 percent of people surveyed never or rarely dreamed in color, but in 1942 as many as 71 percent never or rarely had. It's amazing the difference TV and movies have made!

Answer on page 178.

Current Events

GENERAL KNOWLEDGE | LANGUAGE

1	2	3	4	5	■	6	7	8	■	9	10	11
12					■	13			■	14		
15					16				17			
18							■	■	19			
■	■	20				■	21	22		■	■	■
23	24			■	25	26			■	27	28	29
30				31					32			
33			■	34				■	35			
■	■	■	36			■	37	38			■	■
39	40	41		■	■	42					43	44
45				46	47							
48			■	49			■	50				
51			■	52			■	53				

ACROSS

1. Some Japanese cartoons
6. Triangular sail
9. Water purity org.
12. Clutch, perhaps
13. Rare sighting
14. Tic follower
15. Deceptive advertising operation
18. Imitated a whale
19. Scouting pledge word
20. B.C. carnivore
21. _______ Paulo, Brazil
23. Movie pig
25. Kind of bar
27. Gives the green light to
30. Like some surveillance systems
33. Trill name on "Star Trek: Deep Space Nine"
34. Having no give

35. Dept. of Justice employee
36. Method
37. Coloring
39. Prosaic
42. Progress hamperer
45. Many a speedster
48. Bran source
49. Prefix with brow
50. Horned creature
51. Word before hill or jumper
52. Kettle and Bell
53. Jobs

DOWN

1. Police band calls: abbr.
2. First quarter moon effect
3. TV, slangily
4. Becomes due
5. Thrill
6. "High Crimes" actress
7. Conditional statements
8. Violin stick
9. Remark to a backstabber
10. Treaty
11. "_______ Breaky Heart"
16. Delivery service promise
17. Groom's reply
21. Skim along a surface
22. Publicize
23. They lead to E
24. Nouvelle Caledonie, e.g.
26. Post-ER stop, possibly
27. Film flubs
28. Model builder's purchase
29. Where slop is served
31. Greek H
32. Sacred composition
36. A question of identity
38. "That is"
39. Super Mario _______
40. Fuel tank problem
41. Play opener
42. Hitter's stats
43. Lift up the wrapping, perhaps
44. Miscalculates
46. Pirate's quaff
47. Recombinant _______

Answers on page 178.

Cross Sums

COMPUTATION PLANNING

Use the numbers below to fill in the grid. Each cell at the top of the 3 adjacent cells is the sum of numbers below it. So, as seen in the example, A=B+C+D.

1 2 3 4 6 7 8 9 14 14 15 16 18 35 37 51 54 55 123 143 160 426

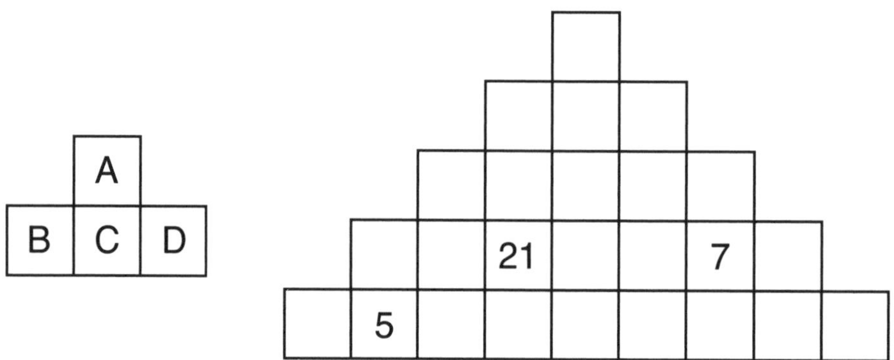

Word Jigsaw

LANGUAGE PLANNING

Fit the pieces into the frame to form common words reading across and down. There's no need to rotate the pieces; they'll fit as shown, with each piece used once.

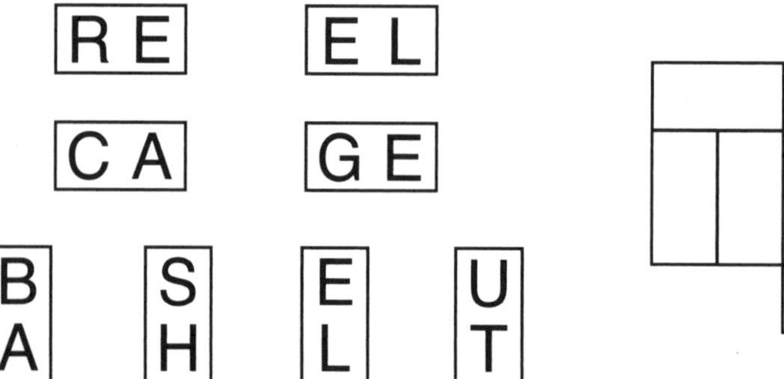

Answers on page 178.

Missing Connections

LANGUAGE **PLANNING**

It's a crossword without the clues! Use the letters below to fill in the empty spaces in the crossword grid. When you are finished, you'll have words that read both across and down, crossword-style.

A A A A B B B E E E E F H H N O O O O O P R R R R S T T T U

Trivia on the Brain

Most people take about 6 seconds to yawn. If you see someone yawn, there's a 55 percent chance you'll also yawn within 5 minutes. What's funnier is that there's a 65 percent chance you'll start yawning soon, just because you've been reading about yawning!

Answer on page 179.

1-2-3

LOGIC PLANNING

Place the numbers 1, 2, and 3 in the circles below. The challenge is to have only these 3 numbers in each connected row and column—no number should repeat. Any combination is allowed.

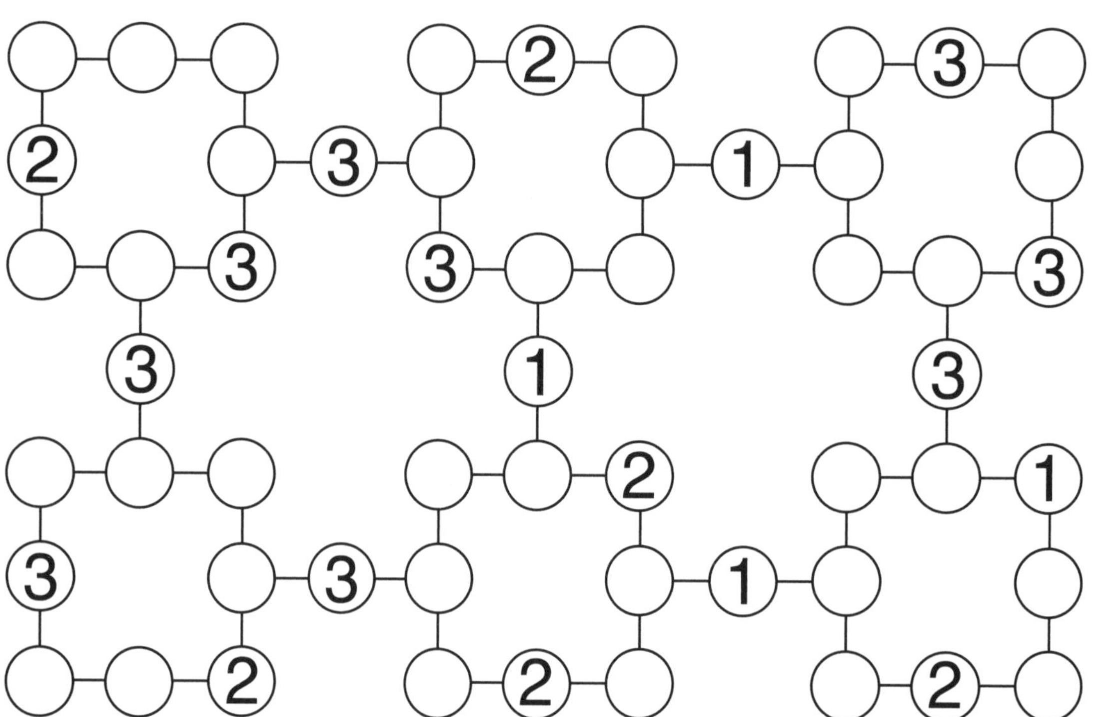

Trivia on the Brain

The human brain is composed of about 400 miles of blood vessels.

Answer on page 179.

From A to Z

ATTENTION VISUAL SEARCH

Every word in this alphabetical list is contained within the letter grid. The words can be found in a straight line horizontally, vertically, or diagonally. They may be read either forward or backward. When you have found all the words, the remaining letters will spell a message.

E	G	J	L	L	A	O	D	G	O	N	G
N	E	E	D	L	E	Q	O	T	I	O	S
O	E	S	A	U	E	E	U	L	Y	N	O
H	U	T	I	N	N	H	O	E	G	O	H
P	E	E	S	K	I	I	S	N	E	I	A
O	L	R	Y	O	V	R	C	F	L	N	T
L	T	W	A	E	M	Y	E	O	I	O	E
Y	S	U	C	A	B	A	B	L	R	S	E
X	I	O	H	G	S	S	C	R	L	N	H
U	H	R	T	L	T	S	A	A	A	A	C
B	W	C	R	E	P	P	I	Z	W	S	B
T	E	G	R	A	T	T	E	K	C	O	R

ABACUS	HAWK	ONION	UNICORN
BALLERINA	IGLOO	PARROT	VIOLIN
CHEETAH	JESTER	QUEEN	WHISTLE
DAISY	KISS	ROCKET	XYLOPHONE
EAGLE	LOBSTER	SHELL	YACHT
FISH	MACAW	TARGET	ZIPPER
GONG	NEEDLE		

Hidden message: ______________________________

Answers on page 179.

Alien Mutations

PLANNING VISUAL LOGIC

Shown are 12 mutation chambers surrounded by alien figures. Each of the 4 aliens on the left passed through the 3 chambers to their right and were transformed into the figures on the other side (e.g. the alien on the left of A passed through chambers A, B, and C, and was mutated into the alien to the right of C). The same goes for the aliens above the chambers; each passed through the 4 chambers directly below them and came out mutated on the other side.

Each chamber affects 1—and only 1—alteration (changes in head or body shape, changes in posture, addition/removal of appendages). Note: Some chambers in the same row or column will undo what a previous chamber has done.

What mutation is each chamber responsible for?

Answers on page 179.

Twenty-four Jumble

ANALYSIS COMPUTATION

Arrange the numbers and signs in this cornucopia to come up with the number 24.

Marbles

ANALYSIS LOGIC

Place 11 marbles into the grid without having any touch one another, not even diagonally. There are some walls, represented by thick lines, that block the view of the marbles. Marbles must not "see" each other in a horizontal or vertical direction. We've placed the first 1 to get you started.

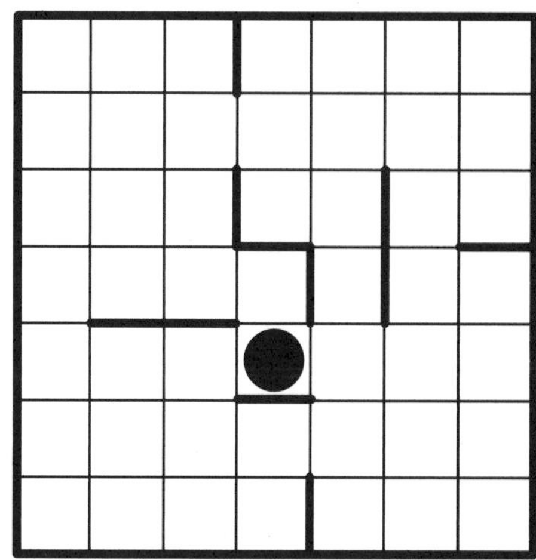

Answers on page 179.

Get It Straight

PLANNING SPATIAL REASONING

Don't get too caught up in all the twists and turns as you negotiate your way to the center of this intricate labyrinth.

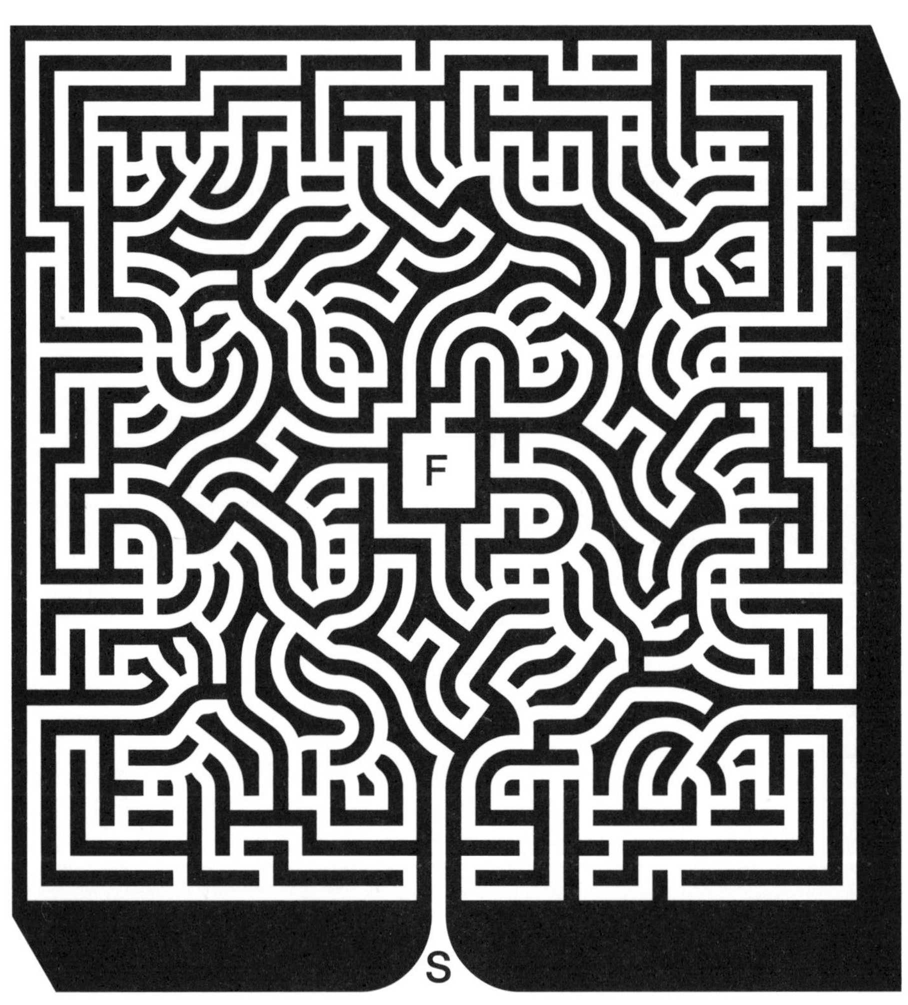

Answer on page 179.

Code-doku

LANGUAGE LOGIC

	H						E	
		R				N		Y
O			R		H			T
R				Y	O			N
			N		L		O	
E				T	J			
N			O		E			H
H		T	Y			J		
	R						L	

Solve this puzzle just as you would a sudoku. Use deductive logic to complete the grid so that each row, column, and 3 by 3 box contains each of the letters EHJLNORTY in some order. The solution is unique.

When you have completed the puzzle, unscramble those 9 letters to reveal America's tenth president.

Answer: ______________________________

Trivia on the Brain

The word "shrink" comes from "head-shrinker" and probably started as a denigrating comparison between psychotherapy and the tribal practice of boiling heads. The first recorded use of the descriptor was in 1966.

Answer on page 179.

L'adder

ANALYSIS COMPUTATION

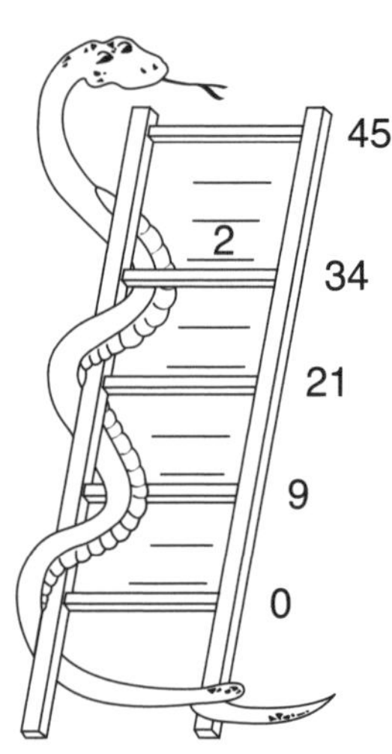

Starting at the bottom rung, use the numbers 1 through 9 to add up to the top number. Numbers can only be used once. There's a catch though: The precise sums must be met along the way.

Cross Sums

COMPUTATION PLANNING

Use the numbers below to fill in the grid. Each cell at the top of the 3 adjacent cells is the sum of numbers below it. So, as seen in the example, A=B+C+D.

1 2 3 4 5 6 6 7 8 11 12 18 20 24 25 35 38 49 84 87 108 279

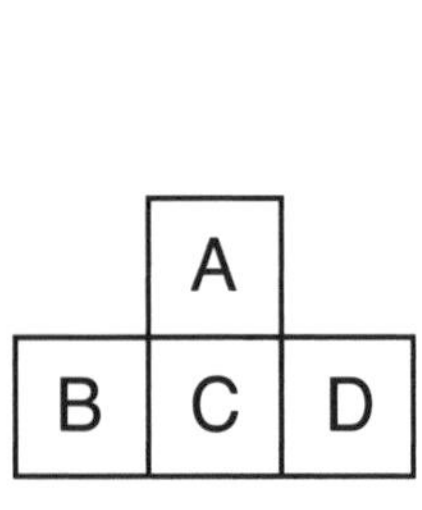

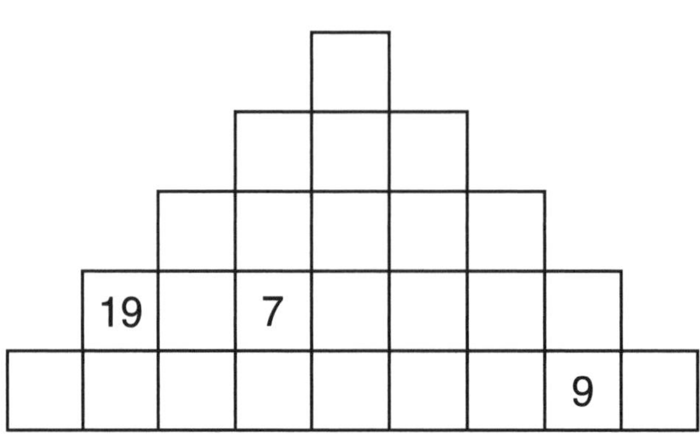

Answers on page 180.

Hashi

PLANNING VISUAL LOGIC

Each circle represents an island, with the number inside indicating the number of bridges connected to it. Draw bridges between islands using the number given, but there can be no more than 2 bridges going in the same direction and there must be a continuous path connecting all islands. Bridges can only be vertical or horizontal and may not cross islands or other bridges. We've drawn some bridges to get you started.

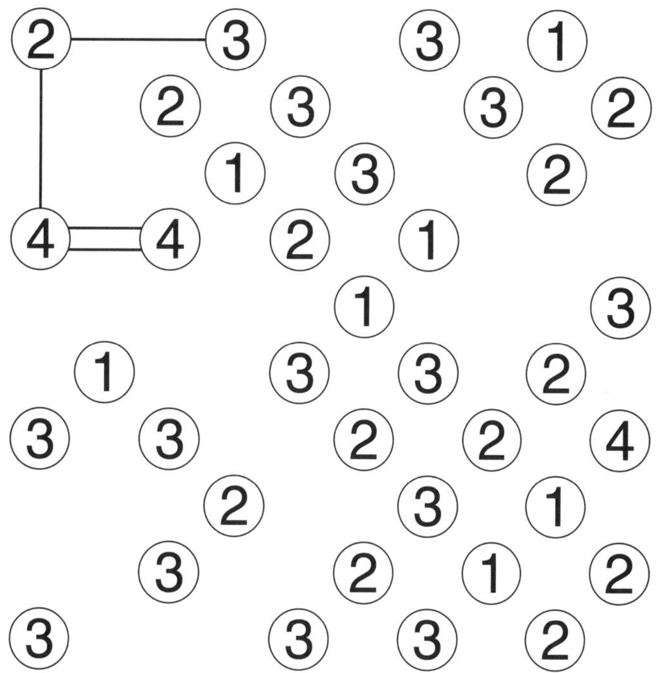

Trivia on the Brain

It takes the average person about 15 minutes to fall asleep.

Answer on page 180.

ABCD

LOGIC PLANNING

Every cell in the grid contains 1 of 4 letters: A, B, C, or D. No letter can be horizontally or vertically adjacent to itself. The tables above and to the left of the grid indicate how many times each letter appears in that column or row. Can you complete the grid?

			A	1	2	2	2	1	1
			B	1	1	2	0	2	3
			C	1	3	0	2	1	2
A	B	C	D	3	0	2	2	2	0
2	1	0	3						
1	2	3	0						
1	2	1	2						
1	1	2	2						
2	3	1	0						
2	0	2	2						

Flip the Cards

ANALYSIS LOGIC

Three cards have been laid out, each marked with a letter or symbol on one side and a number on the other. If you want to make sure that every card with an A has a 3 on the other side, and that no 3 card has a star symbol on the other side, which cards need to be turned over?

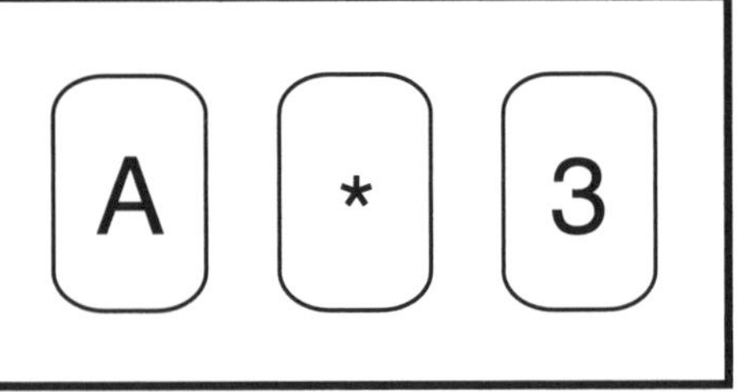

A. All 3 cards

B. The card on the left and the card on the right

C. The card on the right and the card in the middle

D. The card on the left and the card in the middle

Answers on page 180.

Cross Count

COMPUTATION LANGUAGE

1	2	3	4	5	6	7	8	9
A	B	C	D	E	F	G	H	I
J	K	L	M	N	O	P	Q	R
S	T	U	V	W	X	Y	Z	

All the letters of the alphabet have been assigned a value from 1 through 9, as demonstrated in the box on the left. Fill in the grid with common words and/or names so that the rows and columns add up correctly.

				22
		I	I	23
	I			6
	5	5	5	24
21	26	14	14	

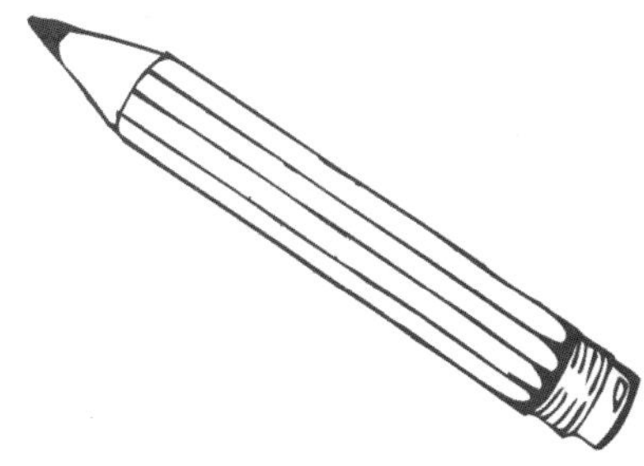

Calcu-doku

COMPUTATION LOGIC

Use arithmetic and deductive logic to complete the grid so that each row and column contains the numbers 1 through 5 in some order. Numbers in each outlined set of squares combine to produce the number in the top corner using the mathematical sign indicated. The solution is unique.

32×		15×	4+	
			11+	2/
3	4-			
3-	6×			4-
		12×		

Answers on page 180.

Word Columns

LANGUAGE PLANNING

Find the hidden quote from Richard Nixon by using the letters directly above each of the blank squares. Each letter is used only once. A black square indicates the end of a word.

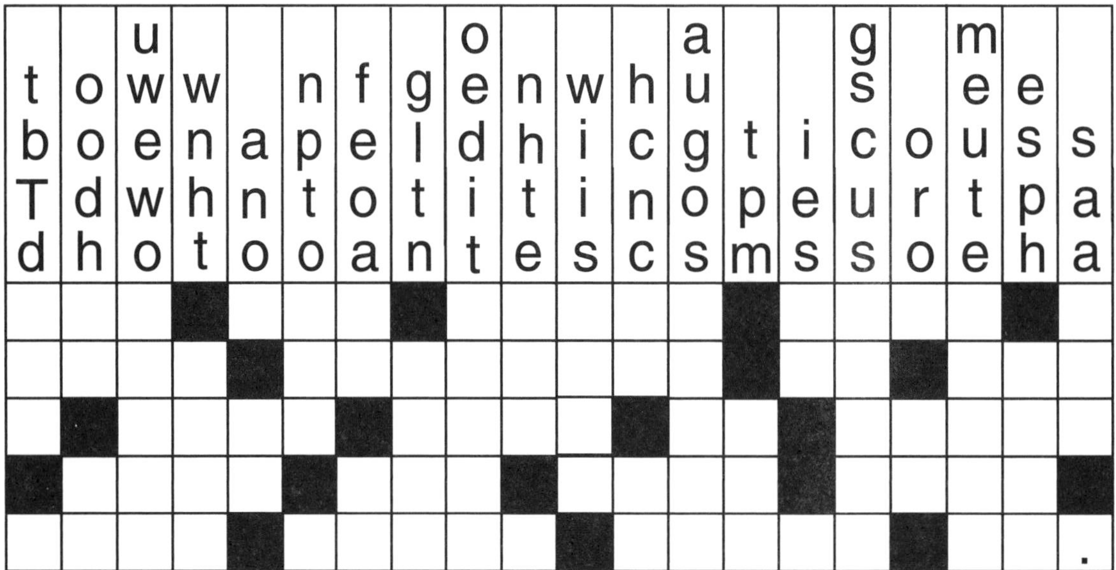

Trivia on the Brain

While crosswords were sweeping the United States during the '20s, Europe stood disapproving. Crosswords were seen as a distraction and were blamed for lower levels of productivity. It wasn't until January 2, 1930, that the first crossword appeared in *The Times* of London with overwhelming support from readers.

Answer on page 180.

Snake Shapes

CREATIVE THINKING | SPATIAL VISUALIZATION | VISUAL LOGIC

Which of the 3 shapes below fit into the grid without overlapping its borders? The shapes may be rotated but not mirrored.

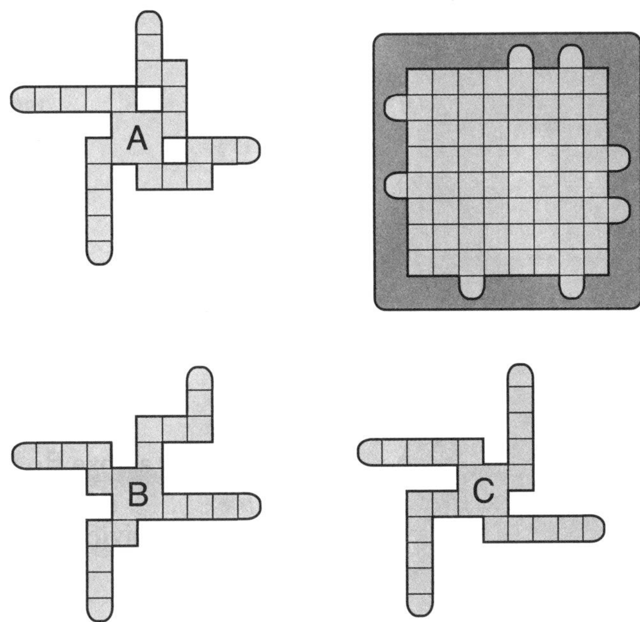

Cast-a-Word

LOGIC | PROBLEM SOLVING

There are 4 dice, and there are different letters of the alphabet on the 6 faces of each of them (each letter appears only once). Random throws of the dice produced the words in this list. Can you figure out which letters appear on each of the 4 dice?

AXED	HUNG	PECK
BUDS	KILT	PLUG
CRIB	LAKE	PUNY
FLOP	MOVE	QUIT
HONE	MULE	VIEW

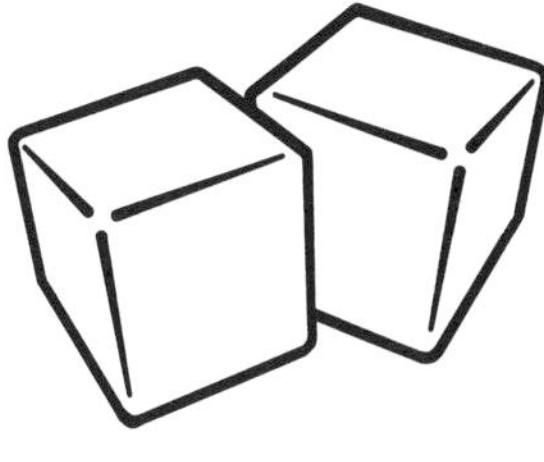

Answers on page 180.

Perfect Score

COMPUTATION **VISUAL LOGIC**

Make 3 successful hits so that the sum of the numbers is 100. Double and triple scores do not apply. Numbers may be used more than once.

Word Jigsaw

LANGUAGE **PLANNING**

Fit the pieces into the frame to form common words reading across and down. There's no need to rotate the pieces; they'll fit as shown, with each piece used once.

RY PE

KI OR

Y/E L/L D/O E/G

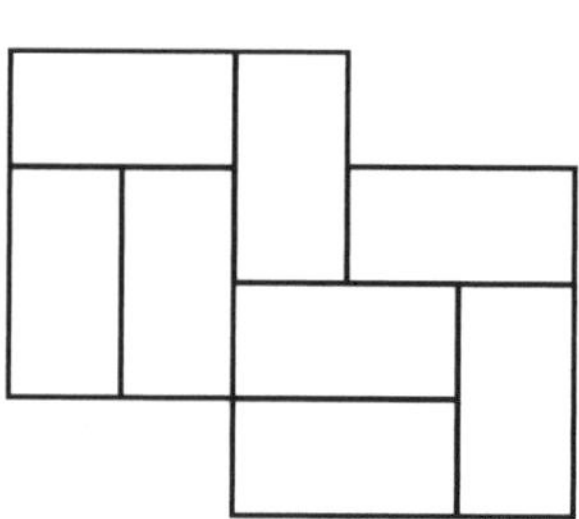

Answers on page 180.

Level 3

Silly Proverbs

LOGIC

Professor Sill E. Sayin made up some proverbs for his next book and has listed them in order of importance. However, he has copied down the words in the wrong order. Although each item is in the correct column, only 1 item in each column is correctly positioned. The following facts are true about the correct order:

1. Demented is 1 place below rhinos and 1 above crowds.

2. Crazy, need, and mud are not second.

3. Avoid is 2 places below ugly.

4. Fame is 2 places below mice and 1 above attack.

5. Spiders is not fourth.

Can you determine the correct order?

	Adjective	Noun 1	Verb	Noun 2
1	crazy	cats	need	lipgloss
2	fat	mice	eat	mud
3	ugly	rhinos	avoid	crowds
4	stinking	fleas	attack	fame
5	demented	spiders	love	pizza

Trivia on the Brain

Famous names are popular words for making anagrams. For example, within "Florence Nightingale" you can find "flit on, cheering angel," and within "Clint Eastwood" you'll find "old west action."

Answer on page 181.

Kakuro

ANALYSIS COMPUTATION

Place a number from 1 through 9 in each empty cell so that the sum of each vertical or horizontal run (rows and columns extending from already numbered cells) equals the number at the top or on the left of that run. Numbers may not be repeated in any run, and runs end at dark-colored squares.

■	■	■	■	↓19	↓11	↓20	■	■	■
■	↓16	↓17	→24				■	↓11	↓13
→17			↓24 →6				↓11 →17		
→27					→11				
■	↓7	↓24 →16			→16			↓15	↓13
→18				■	■	→7			
→12			↓18	■	■	■	↓14 →17		
→17				↓18	■	↓26 →7			
■	↓12	↓8 →3			→17			↓17	↓16
→26					↓3 →28				
→4			→6				→17		
■	■	■	→18				■	■	■

Trivia on the Brain

Arthur Wynne created the first crossword puzzle, which was published in the New York *World* on December 21, 1913.

Answer on page 181.

Identity Parade

ANALYSIS LOGIC

Oops! Four mugshots accidentally got sent through the shredder, and Officer Burns is trying to straighten them out. Currently, only 1 facial feature in each row is in its correct place. Officer Burns knows that:

1. C's nose is 1 place to the left of D's mouth.
2. C's eyes are 1 place to the right of C's hair.
3. B's nose is not next to C's nose.
4. A's eyes are 2 places to the left of A's mouth.
5. C's eyes are not next to A's eyes.
6. D's hair is 1 place to the right of B's nose.

Can you find the correct hair, eyes, nose, and mouth for each person?

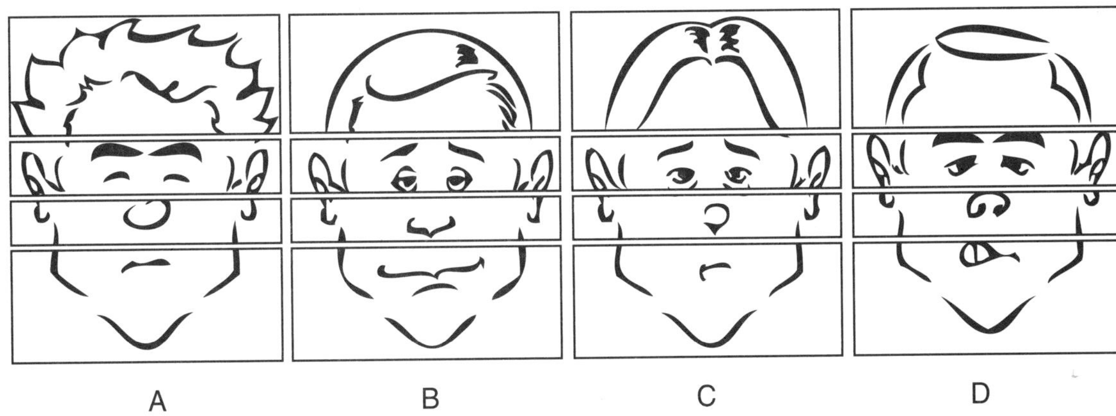

Answer on page 181.

Digital Sudoku

LOGIC

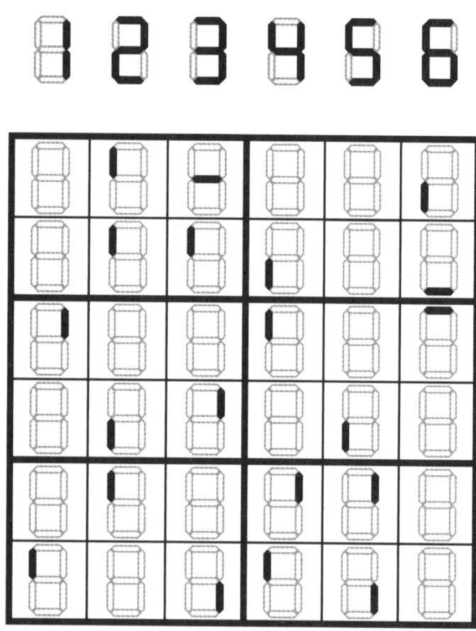

Use deductive logic to complete the grid so that each row, each column, and each 3 by 2 box contains the numbers 1 through 6 in some order. Some segments have already been filled in. The solution is unique.

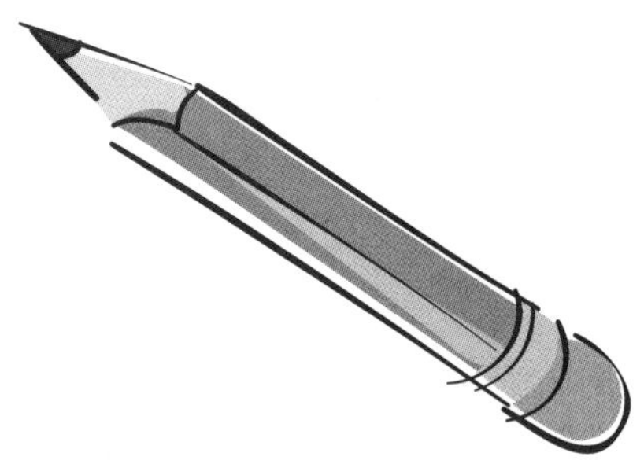

Break the Code

COMPUTATION LOGIC

Determine the value of the symbols, and find the missing number (the sum of the symbols diagonally).

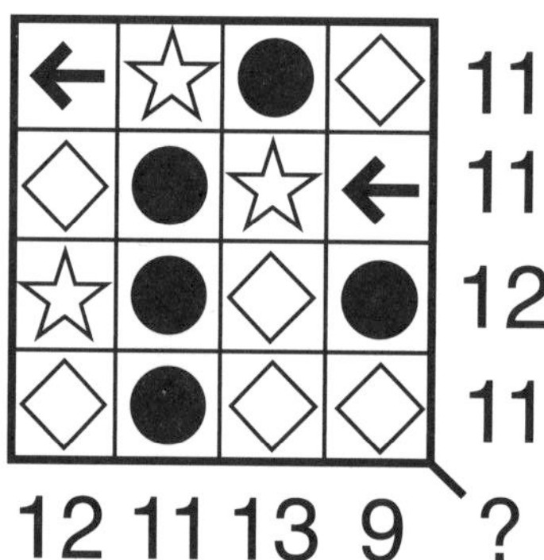

Answers on page 181.

Codeword

ANALYSIS LANGUAGE

Each letter of the alphabet is hidden in code: They are represented by a random number from 1 through 26. With the letters already given, complete the crossword puzzle with common English words and break the code.

15	10	17	11	11	18	■	■	12	■	6	2	12
■	17	■	■	17	■	16	5	4	24	23	■	2
12	17	5	17	3	3	17	■	12	■	5	■	15
■	15	■	■	19	■	4	■	4	10	21	17	15
11	23	5	12	23	4	21	23	■	■	2	■	2
■	13	■	■	21	■	15	■	17	■	16	■	10
2	15	15	7	23	15	■	23	13	3	17	22	23
13	■	21	■	22	■	26	■	21	■	■	23	■
1	■	5	■	■	8	17	21	26	23	5	23	22
23	14	2	21	15	■	21	■	23	■	■	11	■
5	■	6	■	21	■	23	13	9	17	18	23	22
13	■	23	25	7	4	10	■	17	■	■	13	■
17	20	13	■	8	■	■	17	8	21	7	15	23

A B C D E F G H I J K L M N O P Q R S T U V W X Y Z

1	2	3	4	5	6	7	8	9	10	11	12	13

14	15	16	17	18	19	20	21	22	23	24	25	26
	S		O		K							

Answer on page 181.

International Scramblegram

LANGUAGE

Four 11-letter words, all of which revolve around the same theme, have been jumbled. Unscramble each word and write the answer in the accompanying space. Next, transfer the letters in the shaded boxes into the shaded keyword space below and unscramble the 9-letter word that goes with the theme. The theme for this puzzle is countries.

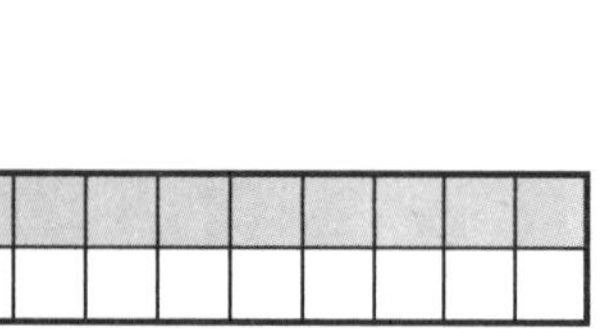

Vex-a-Gon

CREATIVE THINKING

PLANNING

Place the numbers 1 through 6 into the triangles of each hexagon. The numbers may be in any order but they do not repeat within each hexagon shape.

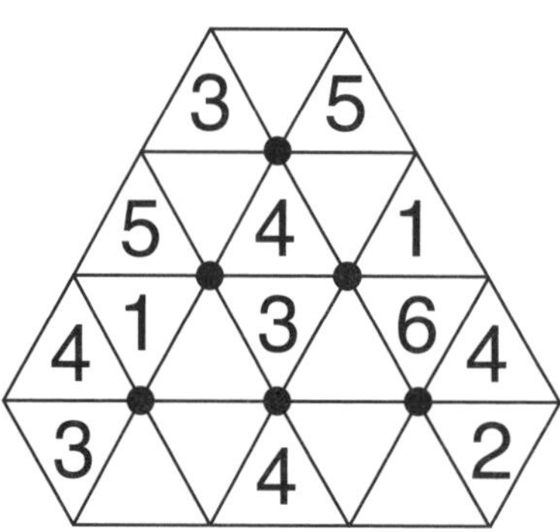

Answers on page 181.

Digitally Mastered

ANALYSIS COMPUTATION

Fill in this crossword with numbers instead of letters. Use the clues to determine which of the numbers 1 through 8 belongs in each square. No zeros are used.

ACROSS

1. Three different even digits such that the third digit is the sum of its first 2 digits
4. Consecutive digits, ascending
6. Consecutive digits, in some order
7. Its third digit is the sum of its first 2 digits

DOWN

1. Its first digit is the sum of its last 2 digits
2. A palindrome
3. The sum of its first 2 digits is equal to the 2-digit number formed by its last 2 digits
5. A square

Minesweeper

ANALYSIS LOGIC

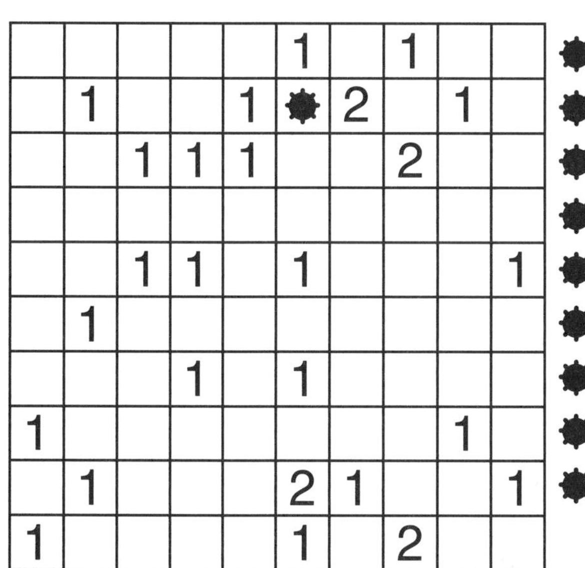

There are 10 mines hidden in the grid. Numbers indicate the number of mines adjacent to that square, horizontally, vertically, and diagonally. We've placed the first 1 to get you started.

Answers on page 182.

The Yellow-Brick Road

ANALYSIS LOGIC

The yellow-brick road splits into the green- and the red-brick roads, which lead respectively to the green city and the red city. In one of these cities, everyone tells the truth, and in the other everyone lies. You want to get to the city of truth. Two people are waiting at the fork in the road, 1 from each city. You can ask one of them 1 question. What is it?

Cluster

ANALYSIS COMPUTATION

Fill in each grape so the number in descending rows is the total of the neighboring numbers from the row above it. Each grape contains a positive whole number. Numbers can be repeated.

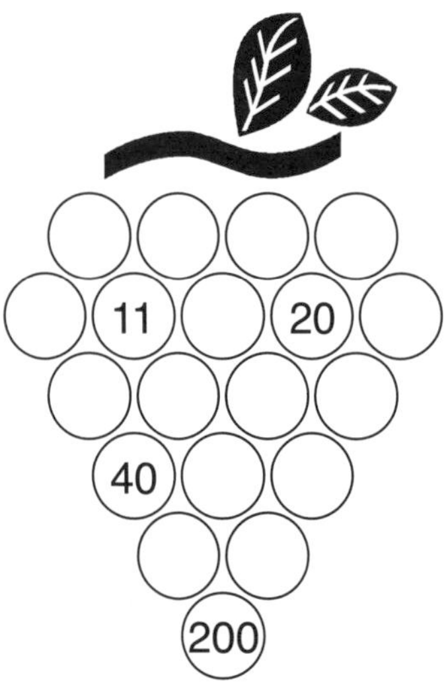

Answers on page 182.

T-Cubed Rectangles

SPATIAL VISUALIZATION · CREATIVE THINKING · VISUAL LOGIC

Four folding patterns are scattered around the cube shown below. Determine which 2 patterns form a cube when folded along the lines. No parts of the cube should overlap.

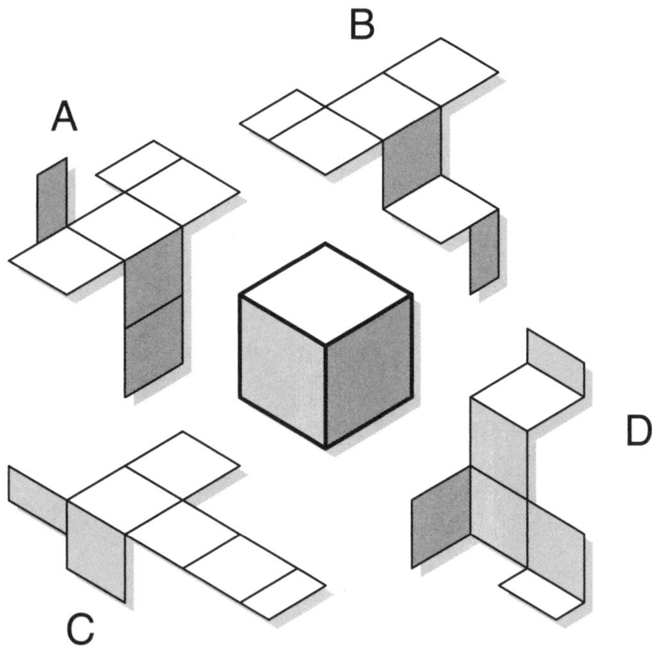

Famous Family Sequence

ANALYSIS · CREATIVE THINKING

Can you complete the sequence below?

C, H, G, G, ___

Answers on page 182.

Petal Puzzle

GENERAL KNOWLEDGE | LANGUAGE

In this petal puzzle, the answers to the clues on the following page read in a curve, from the number on the outside toward the center of the flower. Each number has 2 5-letter answers; one goes in a clockwise direction and the other in a counterclockwise direction. Number 1 clockwise and counterclockwise have been filled in to get you started.

Answers on pages 182.

CLOCKWISE

1. Gaseous glow
2. Printing machine
3. Grind teeth
4. Make very happy
5. Fractured
6. Model T starter-upper
7. Trademark
8. Dark goose variety
9. Crucifix
10. Takes a plane
11. Frankenstein's title
12. Wits
13. The Inferno
14. Thick soup
15. 45-degree angle, for example
16. Straighten
17. 1911 Nobelist
18. Sudsy

COUNTERCLOCKWISE

1. Smithy
2. Undecorated
3. Wine fruit
4. Foe
5. Satiated and bored
6. Vulgar
7. Thin soup
8. Car stopper
9. Lifting machine
10. A Sinatra
11. Hair color
12. Torso's narrow point
13. Employs
14. Starting port for Columbus
15. English poet in the States, W. H. ________
16. Measures of land
17. Hints
18. Bridal ________

Calcu-doku

COMPUTATION LOGIC

Use arithmetic and deductive logic to complete the grid so that each row and column contains the numbers 1 through 6 in some order. Numbers in each outlined set of squares combine to produce the number in the top corner using the mathematical sign indicated. The solution is unique.

1-		3×		10+	
3/		5	4		
3×	5×		10+		2
	6+		5+	30×	
2/	4+	15+		6×	15×

Answer on page 182.

Black Diamonds

COMPUTATION LOGIC

Place the numbers 1 through 4 into the cells of each of the squares below. There's a catch though: Overlapping squares must add up to the number given in each of the black diamonds they form.

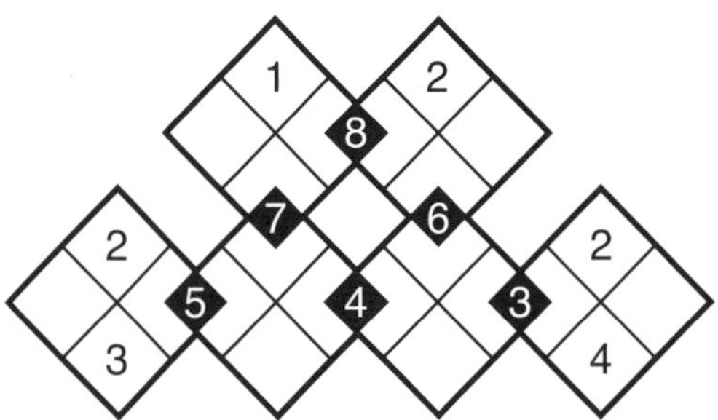

XOXO

ANALYSIS VISUAL LOGIC

Place either an X or an O inside each empty cell of the grid so that there appears no row, column, or diagonal with 4 consecutive cells with the same letter.

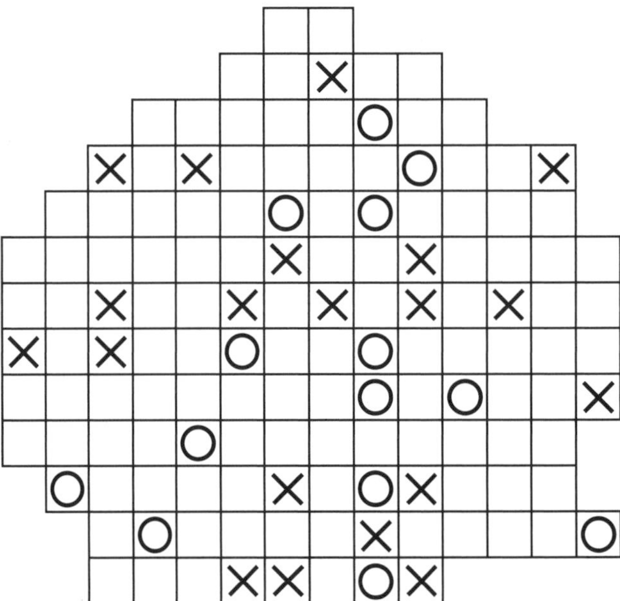

Answers on page 182.

Word Columns

LANGUAGE **PLANNING**

Find the hidden lines of dialogue and cult sci-fi show they're from by using the letters directly below each of the blank squares. Each letter is used only once. A black square indicates the end of a word.

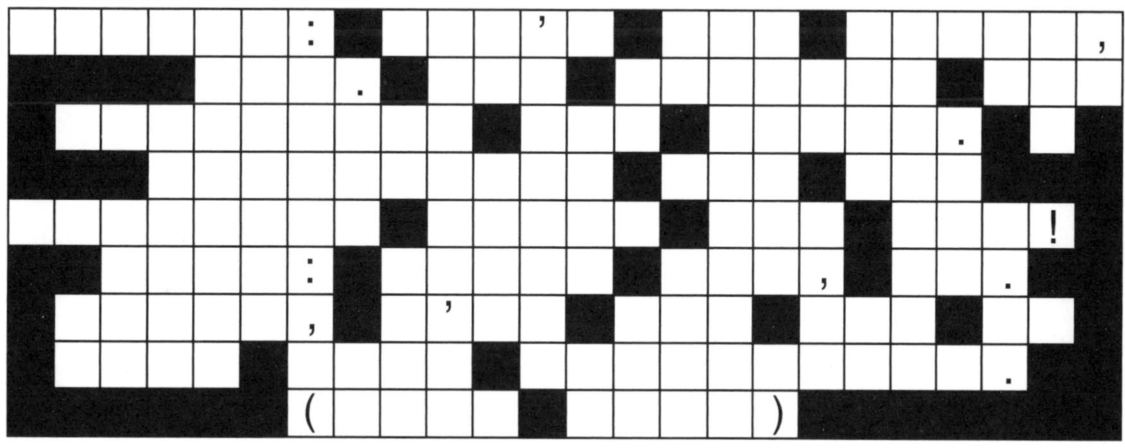

r

o a y y

i s m a h r u T s o t w

u t t i e t z n k s y o d o o

t a i t e r S S n e p s t a s n n y l o

r o o h t e s a A l e e d y n u a t s e a r

a a c r k m p T h o l e d a r l n l h r r A

S S K k e y t t t d a l n r e k u a m M u r s

t c c t n i a h l c l a l r r l e e d t y t o e

Trivia on the Brain

Brothers Matt and Mark Cooley are the creators of the world's largest corn maze. The 2009 *Guinness Book of World Records* claims that their nearly 43 acres of twists and turns is the biggest corn maze in recorded history.

Answer on page 183.

Boost the Challenge

Red, White, Blue, and Green

CREATIVE THINKING LOGIC

Two reds, 2 whites, 2 blues, and 2 greens are to be placed in every row, column, and long diagonal. The following clues will help you place them.

	A	B	C	D	E	F	G	H
1								
2								
3								
4								
5								
6								
7								
8								

1. Two reds, 2 blues, and a white are directly enclosed by the greens.
2. The blues are directly enclosed by the greens; the reds are adjacent.
3. No clue given.
4. Each blue is immediately left of each green.
5. The blues cannot be found in cells A, B, C, or D.
6. No clue given.
7. Each white is immediately right of each green.
8. The greens cannot be found in cells A, B, C, or D.

A. Two whites and 2 reds are directly enclosed by the greens.
B. Two whites and 2 blues are directly enclosed by the greens.
C. No clue given.
D. Two reds and a blue are directly enclosed by the greens.
E. No clue given.
F. The pattern of colors takes the form abcdadbc.
G. Two blues, a red, and a white are directly enclosed by the greens.
H. The greens are directly enclosed by the reds.

Answer on page 183.

Kakuro

ANALYSIS COMPUTATION

Place a number from 1 through 9 in each empty cell so that the sum of each vertical or horizontal run (rows and columns extending from already numbered cells) equals the number at the top or on the left of that run. Numbers may not be repeated in any run, and runs end at dark-colored squares.

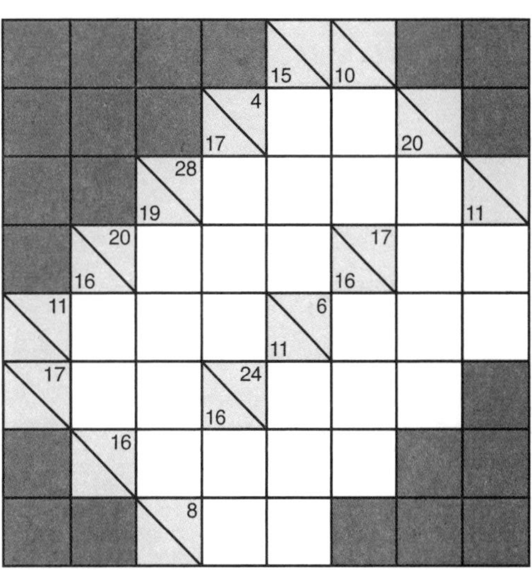

Fitting Words

GENERAL KNOWLEDGE PLANNING

In this miniature crossword, the clues are listed randomly and are numbered for convenience only. It is up to you to figure out the placement of the 9 answers. To help you, we've inserted one letter in the grid, and this is the only occurrence of that letter in the puzzle.

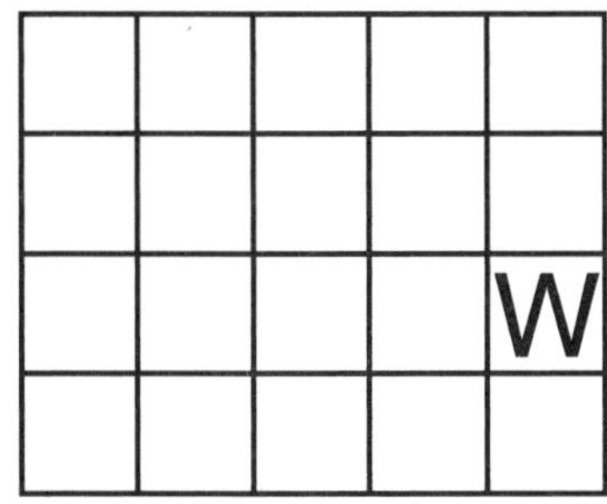

Clues

1. Napoleon's punishment, twice
2. Exams
3. Coagulate
4. Wheel shaft
5. Imagination
6. Berry-bearing evergreens
7. Nudge rudely
8. Penpoints
9. Shoe inserts?

Answers on page 183.

Cross-Math

COMPUTATION PLANNING

	+		×		=	24
×		+		+		
	+		-		=	6
+		-		×		
	-		×		=	24
=		=		=		
24		5		24		

Place the digits 1 through 9 in the empty white squares so that the 3 horizontal and 3 vertical equations are true. Each digit will be used exactly once. Calculations are done from left to right and from top to bottom.

Liar's Logic!

ANALYSIS LOGIC

Use the following information to find out who is lying and who is telling the truth. There are 3 truth-tellers, and 2 liars.

A. B is named Bernie and I'm Alf.

B. C is named Colin and I'm Bernie.

C. D is named Donald and I'm Carl.

D. E is named Eli and I'm Dan.

E. C is named Carl and I'm Ed.

Who are the liars, and whose name(s) can we be sure of, if any?

Answers on page 183.

Mixed-up Marriages

LOGIC

On Saturday, 6 marriages are due to be performed throughout the day at the local church. However, the details of the brides and grooms have been inadvertently mixed up in the planner. Although each name is in the correct column, only 1 name in each column is correctly positioned. The following facts are certain about the correct order:

	Groom 1st	Groom 2nd	Bride 1st	Bride 2nd
1	Abe	Goliath	Minnie	Stephens
2	Bill	Holderness	Nina	Tallis
3	Colin	Idi	Olive	Underwood
4	Doug	James	Pauline	Vitori
5	Eddie	Kite	Alice	Wells
6	Fred	Leonard	Rosie	Yates

1. Yates is 2 places below Goliath.

2. Colin is 1 place below Idi.

3. Fred is 3 places below Nina, who is 2 above Underwood.

4. Vitori is somewhere below Olive who is somewhere below Kite.

5. James is 1 place above Pauline, who is 2 places above Doug.

6. Rosie is 1 place above Abe who is one above Stephens.

Can you give the first and last names of the groom and bride for each position?

Trivia on the Brain

Your amygdala is responsible for generating negative emotions such as anger, sadness, fear, and disgust. To be happy, that part of your brain must be kept quiet. Working on nonemotional mental tasks inhibits the amygdala, which is why keeping yourself busy can cheer you up when you're feeling down.

Answer on page 183.

Hamster Treadmill

CREATIVE THINKING | SPATIAL VISUALIZATION | VISUAL LOGIC

When the hamster starts running on the treadmill, will the needle on the speedometer turn clockwise or counterclockwise?

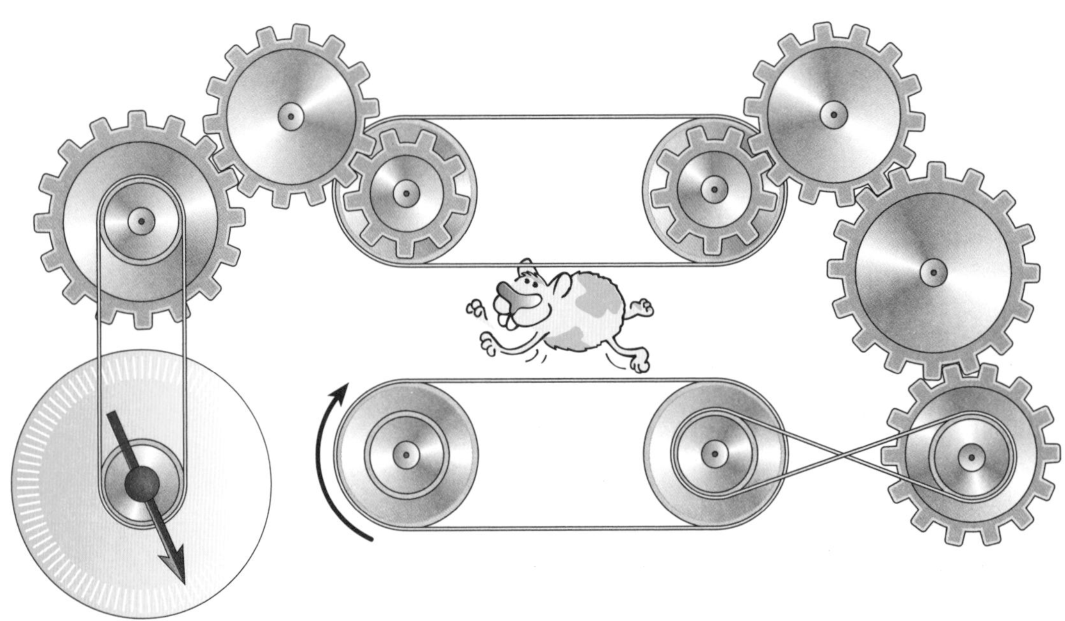

Trivia on the Brain

People continue to debate what the most difficult puzzle is. Unfortunately, they will likely never agree because a puzzle that is difficult for one person may be easier for another.

Answer on page 183.

Arrow Web

ANALYSIS **LOGIC**

Shade in some of the arrows so that each arrow in the grid points to exactly 1 shaded arrow.

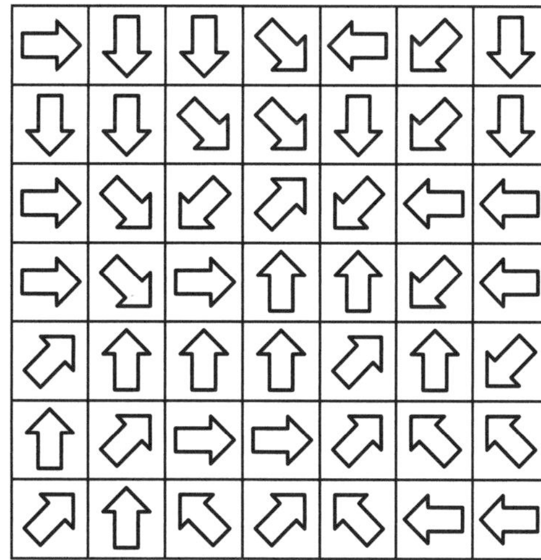

Circular Memory (Part I)

MEMORY

Study the figures below for 1 minute, then wait 1 more minute before turning the page for a memory challenge.

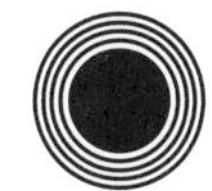       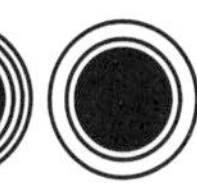 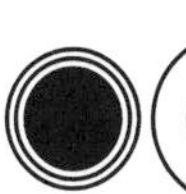 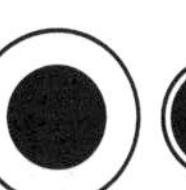

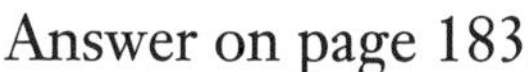
Answer on page 183.

Circular Memory (Part II)

MEMORY

(Do not read this until you have read the previous page!)

Which pair of figures appeared next to each other in the same order, twice?

A. 

B. 

C.  

D.

E. 

Spell Math!

ANALYSIS COMPUTATION

Spell out numbers in the blanks below to obtain the correct solution. Numbers are used only once and range from 1 to 20. A letter has been given to get you started.

___ ___ ___ + ___ ___ ___ ___ ___ = t ___ ___ ___ ___ ___ ___ ___

Answers on page 183.

Codeword

ANALYSIS LANGUAGE

Each letter of the alphabet is hidden in code: They are represented by a random number from 1 through 26. With the letters already given, complete the crossword puzzle with common English words and break the code.

3	24	9	15	8	2	■	23	9	15	12	10	10
24	■	8	■	3	■	23	■	8	■	17	■	15
23	4	15	26	24	2	13	■	3	■	26	■	24
20	■	15	■	11	■	20	13	17	11	8	2	23
4	9	24	26	23	■	10	■	20	■	■	■	16
6	■	26	■	■	■	24	■	13	2	14	8	6
■	■	8	■	4	26	3	24	21	■	12	■	■
20	6	15	24	9	■	17	■	■	■	26	■	23
24	■	■	■	25	■	8	■	3	24	1	5	11
4	19	13	2	12	13	23	■	4	■	3	■	15
24	■	3	■	24	■	13	19	24	20	13	6	13
23	■	24	■	15	■	26	■	22	■	2	■	18
13	4	15	2	13	15	■	7	13	4	11	13	2

A B C D E F G H I J K L M N O P Q R S T U V W X Y Z

1	2	3	4	5	6	7	8	9	10	11	12	13
		M			Y	B						

14	15	16	17	18	19	20	21	22	23	24	25	26

Answer on page 184.

Sudoku

LOGIC

5							4	6
			1	5			2	
	2		6					1
			3					7
		5				8		
8					7			
6					2		7	
	8			7	4			
7	1							4

Use deductive logic to complete the grid so that each row, each column, and each 3 by 3 box contains the numbers 1 through 9 in some order. The solution is unique.

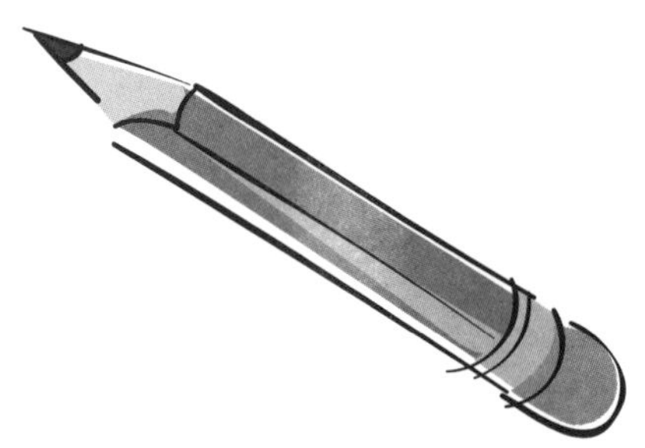

Age Quandary

ANALYSIS COMPUTATION

In 12 year's time, the combined age of my 4 nieces will be 94. What will it be in 5 year's time?

Answers on page 184.

Find It

ATTENTION | VISUAL SEARCH

This is a word search with an added twist. Instead of giving you a list of words to find, we've provided a list of categories. Your challenge is to find 3 items for each category within the group of letters. The words can be found horizontally, vertically, or diagonally. They may read either backward or forward.

3 beverages

____

____

____

3 countries that start with B

____

____

____

3 Harry Potter characters

____

____

____

3 names for strong winds

____

____

____

3 dairy items

____

____

____

O	M	P	B	C	R	E	A	M	C
F	U	L	L	A	C	I	N	E	H
H	I	K	O	O	V	R	A	S	T
E	G	D	L	I	R	C	A	E	N
R	L	A	L	A	C	B	T	E	S
M	E	O	N	O	R	R	N	H	I
I	B	J	F	A	U	T	A	C	M
O	Q	F	Z	G	U	R	S	W	O
N	E	I	O	W	R	N	V	I	O
E	L	Y	V	Y	S	J	U	R	M

Answers on page 184.

Hashi

PLANNING VISUAL LOGIC

Each circle represents an island, with the number inside indicating the number of bridges connected to it. Draw bridges between islands using the number given, but there can be no more than 2 bridges going in the same direction and there must be a continuous path connecting all islands. Bridges can only be vertical or horizontal and may not cross islands or other bridges. We've drawn some bridges to get you started.

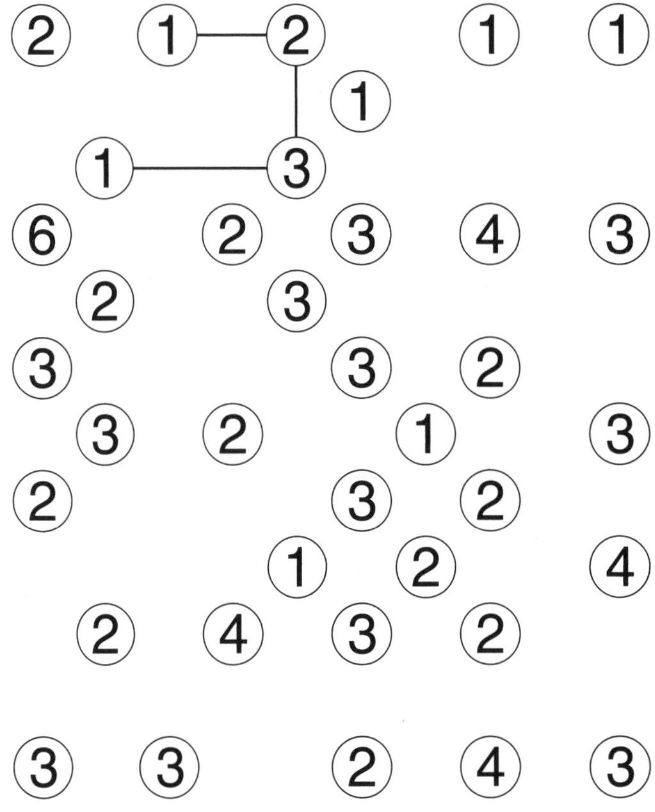

Trivia on the Brain

The brain is the most complex structure in the known universe.

Answer on page 184.

Royal Conundrum

ANALYSIS LOGIC

This person hopes to be a ruler someday. Add an "s" and there are now 2 to choose from. Add another "s" and the person undergoes a gender reassignment. Who is it?

Crypto-Logic

COMPUTATION LOGIC

Each of the numbers in the sequence below represents a letter. Use the mathematical clues to determine which number stands for which letter and reveal the encrypted word.

5 4 0 3 2 4 8 6

Clues:

Put a 1 in front of E and it becomes X	F − 6 = U
X ÷ 2 = F	F − 8 = M
X ÷ 5 = D	F − 2 =N
F + D + 3 = X	D + I = H
F − 1 = I	H + S = 14

Answers on page 184.

Code-doku

LANGUAGE LOGIC

I								
		U		A		O		
			N		D		I	C
	I	A					D	
				U	T			
	E				O		N	
	N		E		I			
		T		O		C		
C							O	

Solve this puzzle just as you would a sudoku. Use deductive logic to complete the grid so that each row, column, and 3 by 3 box contains the letters ACDEINOTU. When you have completed the puzzle, unscramble those 9 letters to reveal something the band Pink Floyd needs none of.

Answer: ______________________

1-2-3

LOGIC PLANNING

Place the numbers 1, 2, and 3 in the circles below. The challenge is to have only these 3 numbers in each connected row and column—no number should repeat. Any combination is allowed.

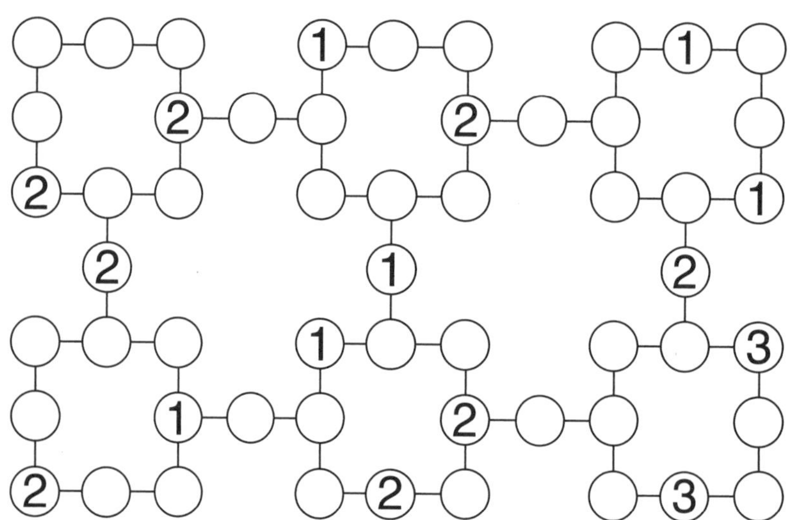

Answers on page 184.

Try Your Luck

PLANNING

SPATIAL REASONING

Don't get too caught up in all the twists and turns as you find your way out of this slot machine.

Answer on page 185.

Star Power

LOGIC **PLANNING**

Fill in each empty square in the grid so that each star is surrounded by the numbers 1 through 8 with no repeats.

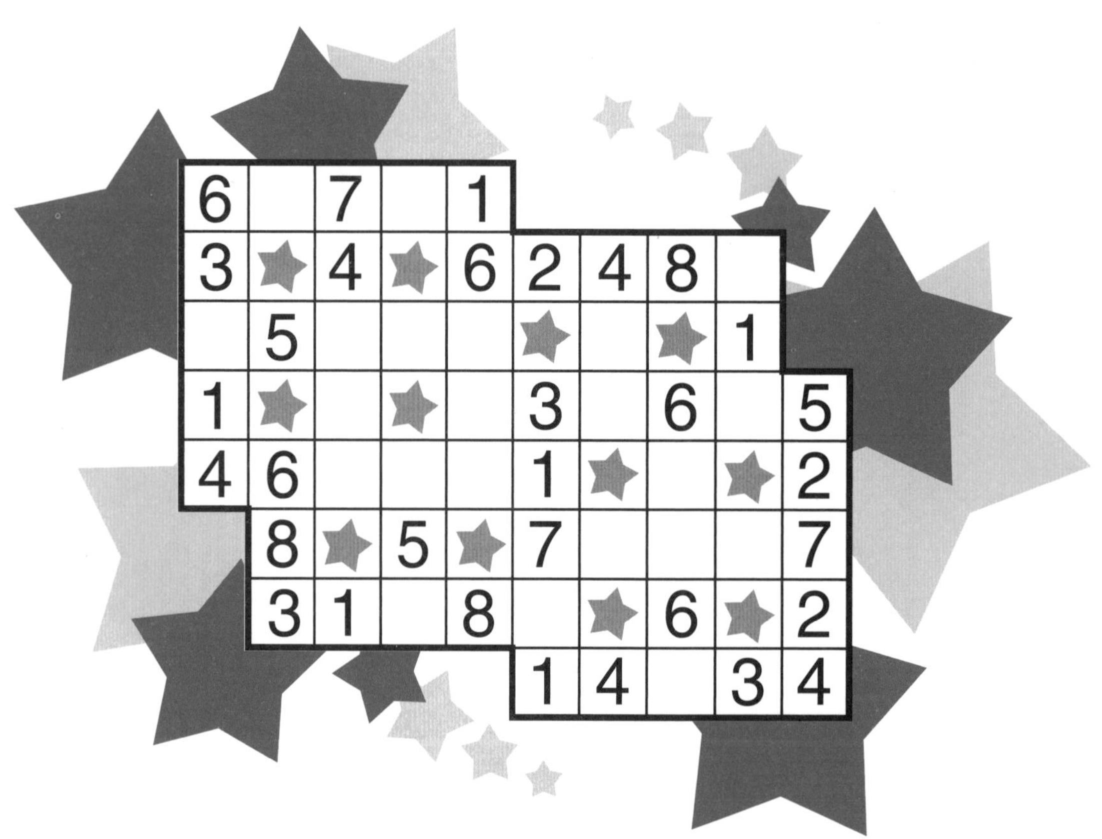

6		7		1					
3	★	4	★	6	2	4	8		
	5				★		★	1	
1	★		★		3		6		5
4	6				1	★		★	2
	8	★	5	★	7				7
	3	1		8		★	6	★	2
					1	4		3	4

Trivia on the Brain

The Dole food company has created the world's largest permanent hedge maze in Hawaii. If you're not careful, you might get lost in the 2.46 miles of paths that make up the maze.

Answer on page 185.

Cross Sums

COMPUTATION PLANNING

Use the numbers below to fill in the grid. Each cell at the top of a cross is the sum of numbers below it. So, as seen in the example, A=B+C+D+E.

1 2 3 4 5 6 8 9

10 11 12 59 60 66

87 126 139 227

519 552 1775

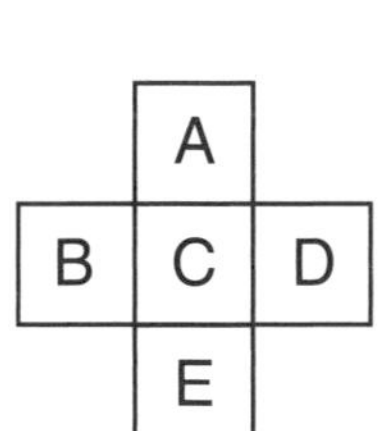

		477				
	65					
			42		7	

Battle Boats

ANALYSIS LOGIC

Place each ship in the fleet located at right within the grid. Ships may be placed horizontally or vertically, but they don't touch each other, not even diagonally. Numbers reveal the ship segments located in that row or column.

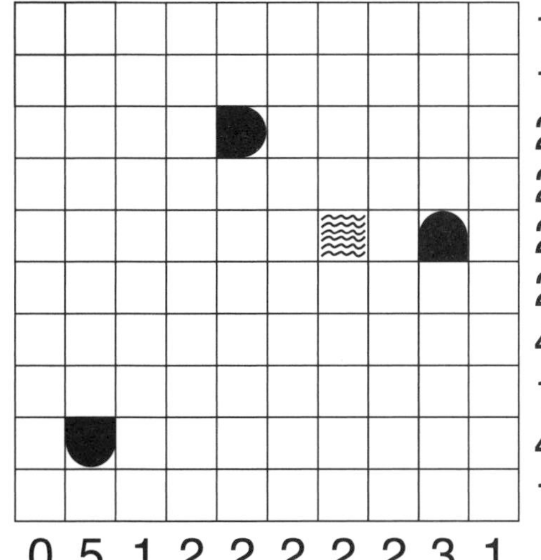

Battleship

Cruisers

Destroyers

Submarines

Answers on page 185.

Boost the Challenge

Be Prepared to Solve This

ATTENTION VISUAL SEARCH

This grid contains terms (found on this page and the next page) associated with Boy Scout merit badges. The words can be found in a straight line horizontally, vertically, or diagonally. They may be read either backward or forward. The leftover letters spell out an additional fact about merit badges.

```
E R O L N A I D N I T H E C U
R O D S S R R N O I T A I V A
A W E K A A R E W E A T H E R
C I N A F E N E R G Y N Y N C
G N T T E N T T O T K U R S H
O G I I T I A G R R A C T T E
D N S N Y C N T O E A L S R R
G I T G L I N W U N T E I A Y
U B R M B D R F O R B A M C R
O M Y M E E R E I O E R E I E
F I U S H M I M E S R S H H T
I L D T T N T M B F H C C P T
P C A A G E A U D L I I T A O
G E S T R O P S E O K E N R P
L I F E S A V I N G I N S G A
A N I M A L S C I E N C E I S
W O O D C A R V I N G E 1 2 1
```

ANIMAL SCIENCE

ARCHERY

ART

AVIATION

CANOEING

CHEMISTRY

CLIMBING

DENTISTRY

DOG CARE

DRAFTING	LIFESAVING	RADIO
ENERGY	MEDICINE	ROWING
FISHING	MUSIC	SAFETY
GOLF	NATURE	SKATING
GRAPHIC ARTS	NUCLEAR SCIENCE	SPORTS
HIKING	PETS	THEATER
INDIAN LORE	PLUMBING	WEATHER
LEATHERWORK	POTTERY	WOOD CARVING

Hidden fact: ____

Fences

ANALYSIS LOGIC

Connect the dots and draw a continuous path that doesn't cross itself. Numbers represent the "fences" created by the path (2 edges are created around the number 2, 3 edges around 3, etc.). We've started the puzzle for you.

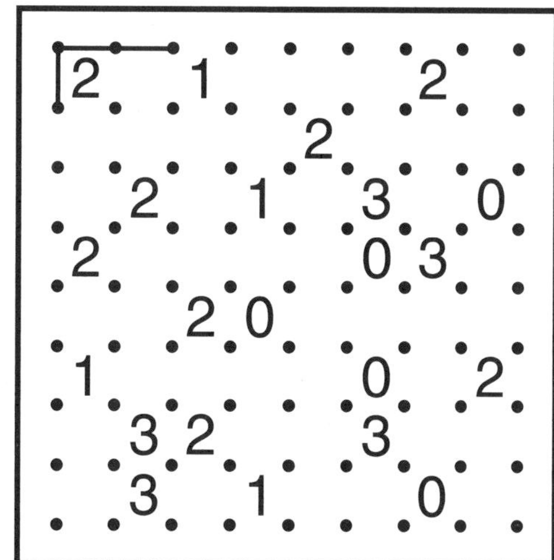

Answers on page 185.

Snake Shapes

CREATIVE THINKING | SPATIAL VISUALIZATION | VISUAL LOGIC

Which of the 3 shapes below fit into the grid without overlapping its borders? The shapes may be rotated but not mirrored.

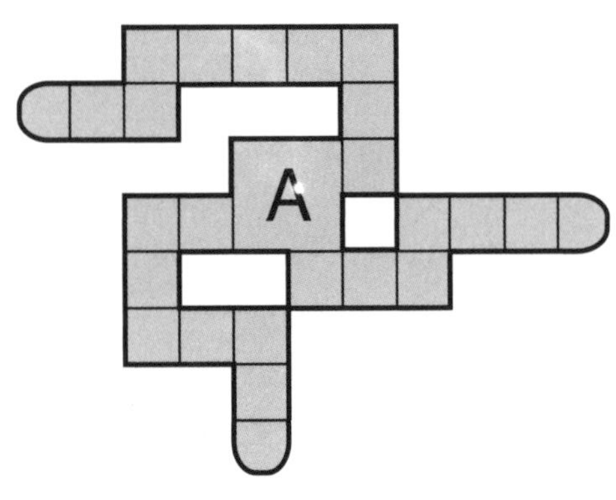

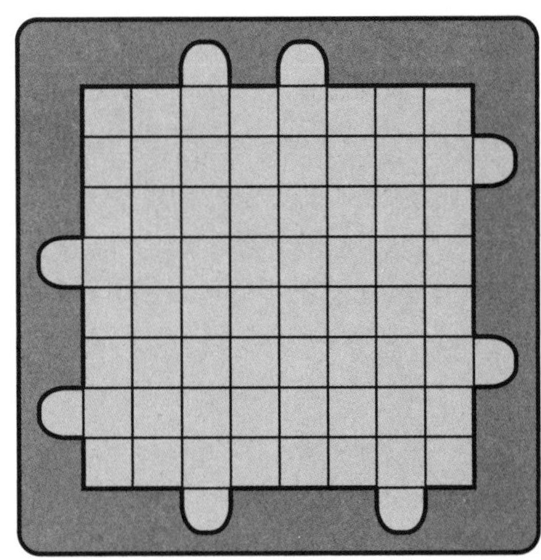

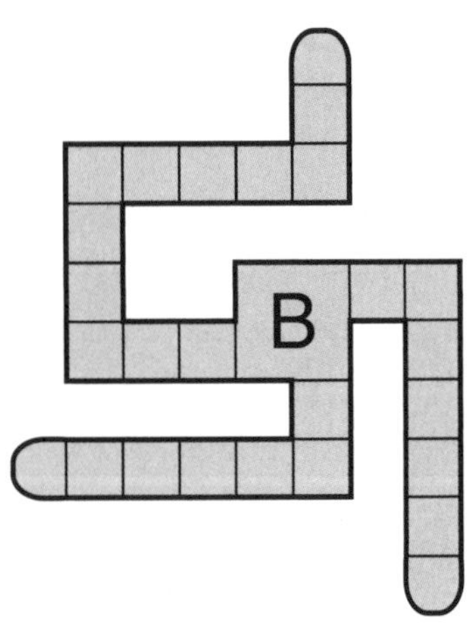

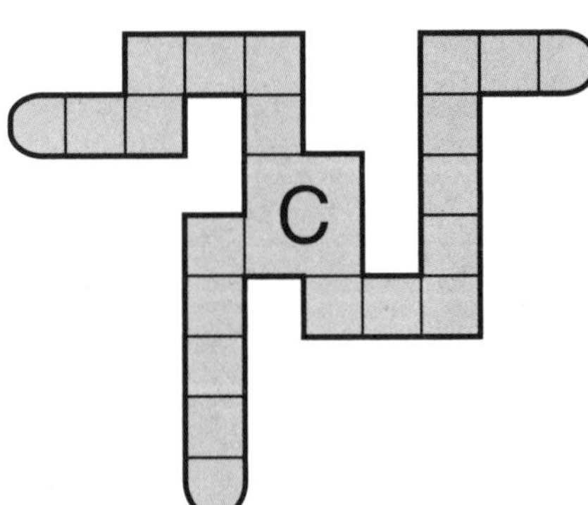

Answer on page 185.

Odd-Even Logidoku

LOGIC PLANNING

The numbers 1 through 9 appear once in every row, column, long diagonal, 3 by 3 grid, and irregular shape. Cells marked with the letter **E** contain even numbers. From the numbers already given, can you complete the puzzle?

Word Ladder

LANGUAGE PLANNING

Use the clues to change just one letter on each line to go from the top word to the bottom word. Do not change the order of the letters. You must have a common English word at each step.

OPINE

________ backbone

____

________ a dramatic rise

____

________ dormant fungus

STORE

Answers on page 186.

Alien Mutations

PLANNING VISUAL LOGIC

Shown are 16 mutation chambers surrounded by alien figures. Each of the 4 aliens on the left passed through the 4 chambers to their right and transformed into the figure on the other side (e.g. the alien on the left of A passed through chambers A, B, C, and D and mutated into the alien to the right of D). The same is true for the aliens above the chambers: Each passed through the 4 chambers directly below them and came out mutated on the other side.

Each chamber affects 1—and only 1—alteration (changes in head or body shape, changes in posture, addition/removal of appendages). Note: Some chambers in the same row or column will undo what a previous chamber has done.

What mutation is each chamber responsible for?

Answers on page 186.

Word Jigsaw

LANGUAGE PLANNING

Fit the pieces into the frame to form common words reading across and down. There's no need to rotate the pieces; they'll fit as shown, with each piece used once.

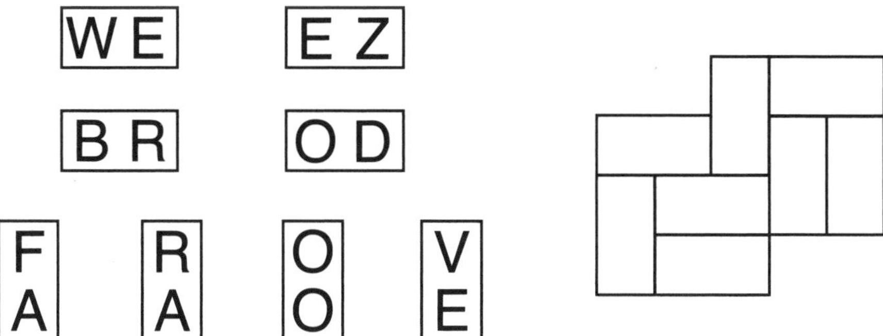

Mastermind

LOGIC

Determine the correct order of the numbers below with the help of the indicators given in each row. A black dot means that a number is in the correct position in that row; a white dot means the correct number is in that row, but in the wrong position. Digits do not appear more than once in the solution, and the solution never begins with 0.

4	0	8	7	6	○ ○
2	3	4	9	7	● ●
1	5	4	7	2	●
7	5	6	0	4	○
?	?	?	?	?	

Answers on page 186.

Clapboard

GENERAL KNOWLEDGE

LANGUAGE

Like a crossword puzzle, the goal here is to find the word or words best suited for the given clues. But unlike a crossword, there are no boxes that separate one word from another. In fact, words on the same line often blend together. The letters ending one word sometimes is the beginning letter of the next, but only on the same line; words never carry over from one row or column to the next.

1	2	3	4	5	6	7	8	9	10	11	12	13
14					15					16 Y		
17					18		19			20 A		
21			22			23		24	25		26	27
28	29		30	31			32			33		
34		35	36		37			38				39
40			41			42	43			44	45	46
47		48	49	50	51		52	53	54			
55	56		57			58	59		60		61	
62		63	64	65		66			67	68		69
70		71		72	73		74					
75				76		77			78			
79					80					81		

ACROSS

1. Kind of party
7. A gear
14. Radio requirements
15. Type of check
16. Jabber
17. Sweet cordial
19. Real ________
21. Tough fiber
22. New Mexico art community
23. Spread oleo
28. Expansive
31. Heavy cart
32. Cravings
33. ________ Lanka
34. Hamburg units
36. Vocalist
38. Perch
40. Speech spot
41. Views
42. Striking beauty
47. Eclectic magazine
49. Fireplace find
52. Spanish king
54. Abominable snowman
55. ________ accompli
57. Score
59. Sweet-potato substitute
60. Ship feature
62. A Gordon
65. Computer for 2001
66. Trails
67. Graf ________
70. Nightmare street
71. Domestic worker
73. Brief swim
74. Malleable
75. Agitates
76. Japanese coin
77. Poetic contraction
78. Violent opposition
79. Prepares rice
80. Had a hunch
81. Actress Joanne

DOWN

1. Used a skewer
2. Sort of eclipse
3. Concord
4. Hostess Perle
5. Moolah
6. "Id ________"
7. Spills the beans
8. Foe
9. Clamp
10. Kett of the comics
11. Showy carpet
12. Cloy
13. Supplemented the hard way
18. Actor Rip
20. Fiery felony
23. Droops
24. Always, in verse
25. Assumed names
26. Scottish Gaelic
27. Morse code entry
29. Lasso
30. Balance sheet items
31. Per ________
32. Even so
33. Scion
35. Diarist Anais
37. Bird's bill
38. Regret
39. Banal
40. Links amateurs
42. Bears' orders
43. Go for the gold?
44. Tide type
45. UFO crew
48. Actress Long
50. Half a fish
51. Grass units
53. Aerie denizens
56. Distribute
59. Jabber
61. Mexicali man
63. Nice friend
64. Casa component
66. Queue
67. Regal address
68. Settled
69. Two of Caesar's final words
72. Distinctive doctrine
74. Sword's foe

Answers on page 186.

Grid Fill

LANGUAGE PLANNING

To complete this puzzle, place the given letters and words into the shapes on this grid. Words and letters will run across, down, and wrap around each shape. When the grid is complete, each row will contain one of the following words: archer, arrest, cookie, on time, slight, Sparta, tamale.

1. C, G, I
2. ET, LI
3. HER, HIM, TEA
4. CART, REAM, SALE, TART
5. ARSON, SPOOK

Trivia on the Brain

In Egypt, Pharaoh Amenemhet III had a maze built within his pyramid to hide his mummified body. He was hoping the maze (which included hidden exits, secret trapdoors, and sliding stones) would confuse tomb robbers. Unfortunately, it didn't work—his tomb was still robbed.

Answer on page 186.

Poetry in Motion

ANALYSIS | PROBLEM SOLVING

The members of Poets Of East Tennessee State (POETS), a college fraternity for poets, found that they had outgrown their old fraternity house and needed a new place for the members to live. The POETS found a brand-new house that was much bigger than their old fraternity house, purchased it, and prepared to move in. The walls of the new hall were flat white and the POETS decided they wanted them painted a different color. The POETS were so creative that they rarely agreed on anything. In fact, the only thing they agreed on is that it would be inappropriate for the walls of their fraternity house to be painted orange, silver, or purple. Why?

Dissection

CREATIVE THINKING | SPATIAL VISUALIZATION | VISUAL LOGIC

Separate the figure into 2 identical parts following the grid lines. The parts may be rotated and/or mirrored.

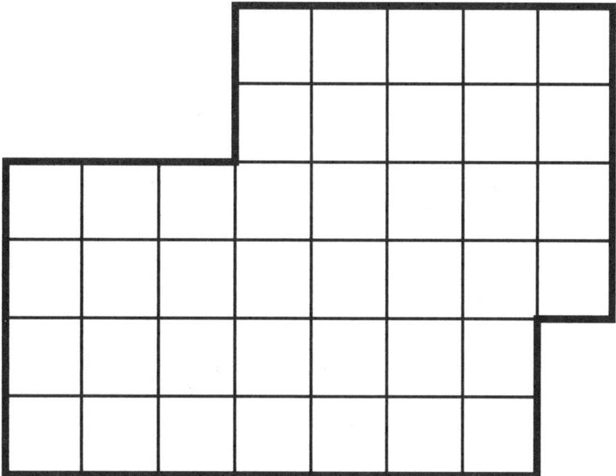

Answers on page 186.

PUSH YOUR MIND TO THE MAX

LEVEL 5

Cross Count

COMPUTATION LANGUAGE

1	2	3	4	5	6	7	8	9
A	B	C	D	E	F	G	H	I
J	K	L	M	N	O	P	Q	R
S	T	U	V	W	X	Y	Z	

All the letters of the alphabet have been assigned a value from 1 through 9, as demonstrated in the box on the left. Fill in the grid with common English words so that the rows and columns add up correctly.

9		p	1	21
		1		13
	9	9		28
9				23
26	24	22	13	

Twenty-four Jumble

ANALYSIS COMPUTATION

Arrange the numbers and signs in this cornucopia to come up with the number 24.

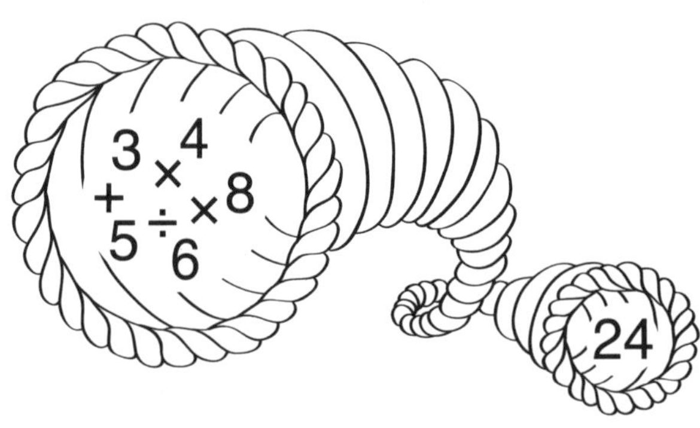

Answers on page 186.

College Baseball by Alpha Sleuth™

LANGUAGE PLANNING

Move each of the letters below into the grid to form common words. You will use each letter once. The letters in the numbered cells of the grid correspond to the letters in the phrase at the bottom. Completing the grid will help you complete the phrase and vice versa. When finished, the grid and phrase will be filled with valid words and you will have used all the letters in the letter set.

Hint: The numbered cells in the grid are arranged alphabetically, so the letter in the cell marked 1 will appear in the alphabet before the letter in the cell marked 2, and so on.

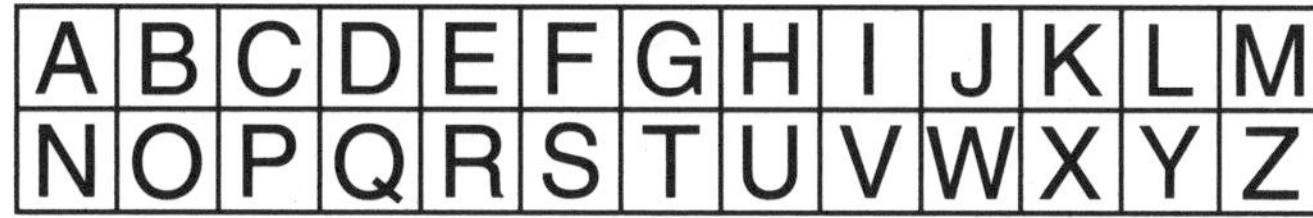

A	B	C	D	E	F	G	H	I	J	K	L	M
N	O	P	Q	R	S	T	U	V	W	X	Y	Z

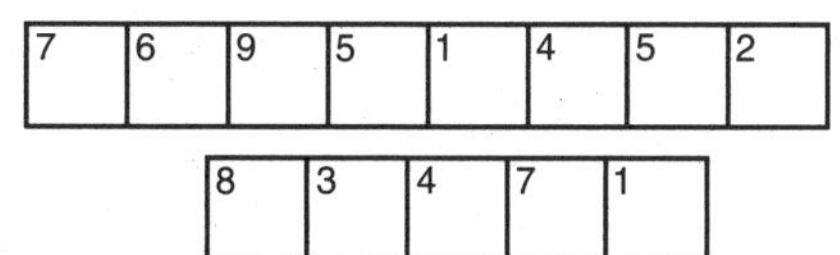

Answer on page 186.

XOXO

ANALYSIS VISUAL LOGIC

Place either an X or an O inside each empty cell of the grid so that there appears no row, column, or diagonal with 4 consecutive cells with the same letter.

Trivia on the Brain

On average, the male brain is slightly bigger than the female brain—but the differences in weight or size don't mean there are differences in mental ability.

Answer on page 187.

Sum Puzzle

COMPUTATION LOGIC

2		4	5	7		3	2
	4	1	6		1	9	
4			1		8	2	4
1	5			5			2
	6	1	3		4	2	6
7	3	4		2	5	1	
	1	6	7	1			2
1		2		3	2	5	

Use the numbers 1 through 9 to fill in the blank squares so that each line, both vertically and horizontally, totals 30.

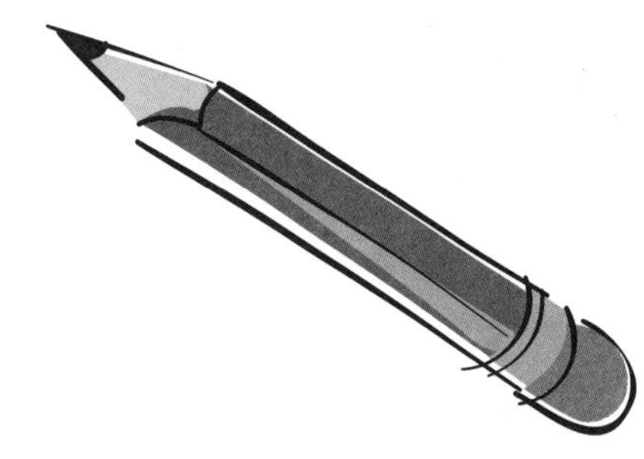

Movie Title and Director Cryptogram

LANGUAGE LOGIC

Cryptograms are messages in substitution code. Break the code to read the film title and its director. For example, THE SMART CAT might become FVO QWGDF JGF if **F** is substituted for **T, V** for **H, O** for **E,** and so on.

1. *KMABL SJ KMABLFTIB*: EPWATR LNBOLOMOV

2. *BLT ILNKNKD*: IBEKPTJ VGSANOV

3. *ONBNWTK VEKT*: MAIMK FTPPTI

4. *AEDNKND SGPP*: XEABNK IOMAITIT

Answers on page 187.

Kakuro

ANALYSIS COMPUTATION

Place a number from 1 through 9 in each empty cell so that the sum of each vertical or horizontal run (rows and columns extending from already numbered cells) equals the number at the top or on the left of that run. Numbers may not be repeated in any run, and runs end at dark-colored squares.

■	■	■	■	24\	9\	13\	■	■	■
■	13\	15\	\6				■	17\	4\
\15			24\24				11\10		
\29					\14				
■	14\	12\13			\4			19\	7\
\24				■	■	\19			
\4			16\	■	■	■	11\10		
\6				11\	■	26\6			
■	10\	9\12			\16			8\	12\
\22					4\10				
\4			\11				\15		
■	■	■	\15				■	■	■

Trivia on the Brain

Your brain uses fatty acids from fats to create the specialized cells that allow you to think and feel.

Answer on page 187.

Hobby Horse

LANGUAGE

Which of these is NOT an anagram for a pleasant hobby?

A. Roman toys

B. Celery bit

C. Opened inlet

D. Hotel syrup

Marbles

ANALYSIS LOGIC

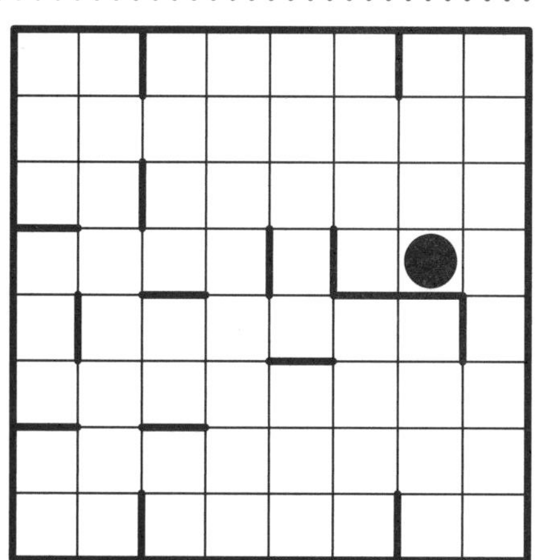

Place 15 marbles into the grid without having any touch one another, not even diagonally. There are some walls, represented by thick lines, that block the view of the marbles. Marbles must not "see" each other in a horizontal or vertical direction. We've placed the first 1 to get you started.

Answers on page 187.

Rhyme Time

GENERAL KNOWLEDGE | LANGUAGE

Each clue leads to a 2-word answer that rhymes, such as BIG PIG or STABLE TABLE. The numbers in parentheses after the clue give the number of letters in each word. For example, "cookware taken from the oven (3, 3)" would be "hot pot."

1. Prime land priced to sell (3, 3): ________________
2. Surfers (3, 3): ________________
3. Perceive a rustle in the woods (4, 4): ________________
4. Wrestler's innovative tactic (4, 4): ________________
5. There's an "a" and a "b" on a 1040 (4, 4): ________________
6. Feature of Saturn (4, 5): ________________
7. Public square in the Middle East (4, 5): ________________
8. Goes overboard in the meat section (5, 5): ________________
9. Get a 10 in a winter Olympic event (5, 5): ________________
10. Demonstrate frustration, in a way (5, 6): ________________
11. Worrisome warble (6, 5): ________________
12. Travel guide's article (6, 6): ________________
13. Accidental sighting (6, 6): ________________
14. Why the mummy wasn't there (7, 7): ________________
15. Sliver from the wooden sled (6, 8): ________________

Answers on page 187.

Sudoku

LOGIC

	3						5	8
8		5		7		1		
					1	2		
			2				8	6
				3				
9	4				5			
		4	3					
		9		4		3		7
6	8						9	

Use deductive logic to complete the grid so that each row, each column, and each 3 by 3 box contains the numbers 1 through 9 in some order. The solution is unique.

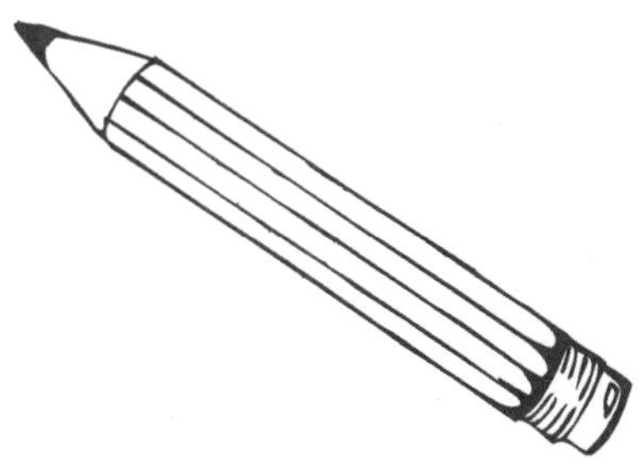

Symbol Value

COMPUTATION LOGIC

Replace the symbols with number values so that the sum of each row, column, and the 1 diagonal add up to the number at the end of each.

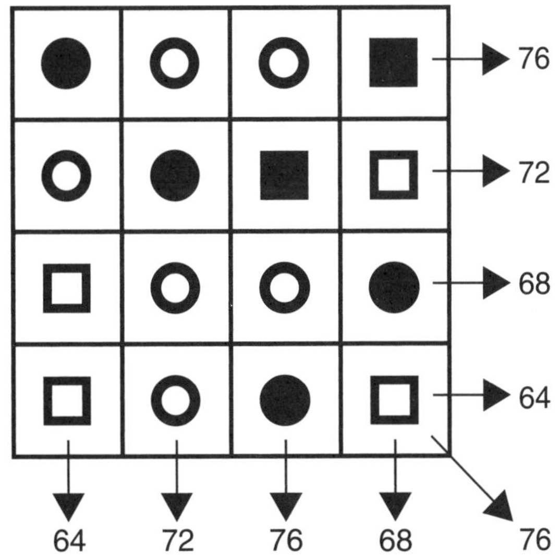

Answers on page 187.

Double Goalposts

GENERAL KNOWLEDGE | LANGUAGE

1	2	3	■	4	5	6	7	■	8	9	10	11
12			■	13				■	14			
15			16					■	17			
■	■	■	18					19				
20	21	22			■	■	■	23				
24				■	25	26	27		■	■	■	■
28				29					30	31	32	33
■	■	■	■	34				■	35			
36	37	38	39		■	■	■	40				
41					42	43	44			■	■	■
45				■	46					47	48	49
50				■	51				■	52		
53				■	54				■	55		

ACROSS

1. Law enforcement alert: abbr.
4. Bogus
8. Cup covers
12. Jeer
13. Slick
14. Provide backup, perhaps
15. Music case
17. Wheat flatbread
18. Astringent medicine
20. He brought about Holy Innocents' Day
23. ________ Mountain Daredevils
24. Tamed
25. Level
28. State of ecstasy

34. Buffoons
35. Cipher
36. Ecstasy
40. Playful animal
41. Rambler
45. Cost of a hand
46. Tuna variety
50. Computer image
51. Fish for
52. Worthless trifle
53. Salamander's cousin
54. Dance in a circle
55. Brume

DOWN

1. Where "Lost" can be found
2. Detachable container
3. Scrape's partner
4. Not hollow
5. Hand guard
6. Actor Guinness of "Star Wars"
7. Legend
8. Highest capital
9. One of the Balearic Islands
10. Get in the way of
11. Tail illegally
16. Stopped sleeping
19. Maximize effectiveness, as a skill
20. British ship letters
21. Big foot?
22. Gun
25. Viscosity symbol
26. Range for some TV broadcasts
27. Sounds of doubt
29. Snack
30. Montezuma, for one
31. Horse doctor
32. Prior to, in poetry
33. "...________ gloom of night..."
36. Site of the pineal gland
37. Tilting tool
38. Following behind
39. What a nose picks up
40. City destroyed in "Godzilla Raids Again"
42. Meat-and-potatoes dish
43. Margarine
44. Over, in Germany
47. Rub out
48. Earth Summit site of 1992
49. Heckler's missile

Answers on page 187.

Get It Straight

PLANNING

SPATIAL REASONING

Don't get too caught up in all the twists and turns as you negotiate your way to the center of this intricate labyrinth.

Answer on page 188.

Elevator Words

GENERAL KNOWLEDGE LANGUAGE

Like an elevator, words move up and down the "floors" of this puzzle. Starting with the first answer, the second word from each answer carries down to become the first word of the following answer. With the clues given, complete the puzzle.

Clue	Answer
1. Certain power station equipment	1. Switch ______
2. Cog	2. ______ ______
3. Dependable worker in a political organization	3. ______ ______
4. Engage in some give and take negotiation	4. ______ ______
5. Like a company's product formula	5. ______ ______
6. Bond's business	6. ______ ______
7. Place to make deliveries	7. ______ Entrance

Famous Anagrams

LANGUAGE

Below are anagrams of 4 famous figures. Which one is NOT an anagram for a famous philosopher?

A. Serenst cedar

B. Sack homonym

C. Atheism resin

D. A milkman tune

Answers on page 188.

Hungry Scramblegram

LANGUAGE

Four 11-letter words, all of which revolve around the same theme, have been jumbled. Unscramble each word, and write the answer in the accompanying space. Next, transfer the letters that are in the shaded boxes into the shaded keyword space below, and unscramble the 9-letter word that goes with the theme. The theme for this puzzle is food.

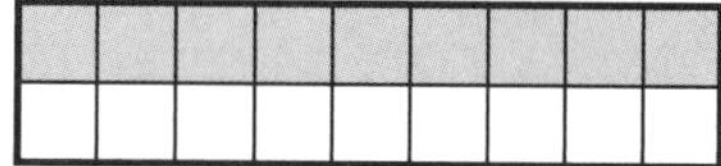

Flip the Cards

ANALYSIS LOGIC

Three cards have been laid out, each are marked with letters on one side and numbers on the other. If you want to make sure that no card with 4s have an S on the other side, and that only cards with 7s have Fs on the other side, which cards need to be turned over?

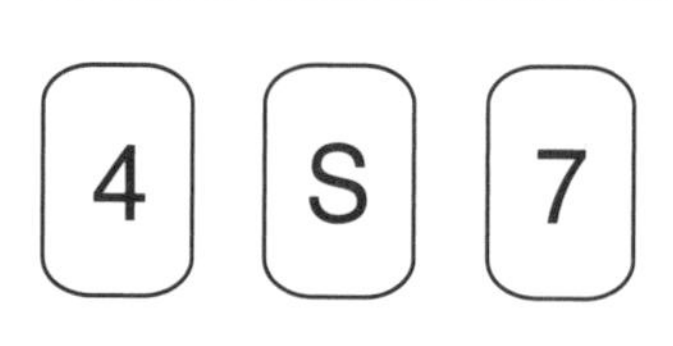

A. All 3 cards

B. The card on the left and the card on the right

C. The card on the right and the card in the middle

D. The card on the left and the card in the middle

Answers on page 188.

ABCD

LOGIC PLANNING

Every cell in the grid contains 1 of 4 letters: A, B, C, or D. No letter can be horizontally or vertically adjacent to itself. The tables above and to the left of the grid indicate how many times each letter appears in that column or row. Can you complete the grid?

			A	2	1	0	2	2	0	1	1	2
			B	0	3	2	0	2	2	2	2	1
			C	1	2	2	2	1	1	2	0	2
A	B	C	D	3	0	2	2	1	3	1	3	1
3	0	3	3									
0	3	1	5									
3	3	2	1								A	
0	3	3	3									
3	3	3	0									
2	2	1	4									

Trivia on the Brain

It's a myth that alcohol destroys brain cells. But it is true that alcohol weakens connections between neurons and makes new cells grow less quickly, which interferes with brain activity and causes serious damage.

Answer on page 188.

Logidoku

LOGIC PLANNING

The numbers 1 through 9 appear once in every row, column, long diagonal, irregular shape (indicated by marked borders), and 3 by 3 grid. With the numbers already provided, can you complete the puzzle?

Minesweeper

ANALYSIS LOGIC

There are 25 mines hidden in the grid. Numbers indicate the number of mines adjacent to that square, horizontally, vertically, and diagonally. We've entered the first 1 to get you started.

	2									✹✹✹
2				1		2	2	2	1	✹✹✹
		2	2				2			✹✹✹
	2			2				1		✹✹✹
			2						1	✹✹
	5	2	2		3			2		✹✹
	✹	2			2	2		1		✹✹
		2						2		✹✹
	3					1				✹✹
1		2		1		1	2		2	✹✹

Answers on page 188.

Acrostic

GENERAL KNOWLEDGE | LANGUAGE

Solve the clues below and then place the letters in their corresponding spots in the grid to reveal a quote from a famous actor. The letter in the upper-right corner of each grid square refers to the clue the letter comes from. A black square indicates the end of a word.

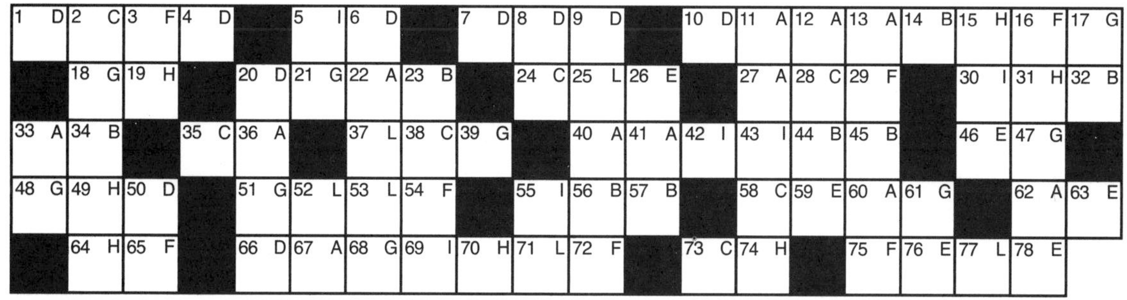

A. Author of quote (2 wds)

__ __ __ __ __ __ __ __ __ __ __ __
40 33 60 11 41 67 12 13 62 36 27 22

B. Keepsake

__ __ __ __ __ __ __ __
34 44 56 32 23 45 14 57

C. Escape artist

__ __ __ __ __ __ __
38 24 28 58 35 2 73

D. Sponge or parasite

__ __ __ __ __ __ __ __ __ __
66 50 9 6 20 1 7 10 4 8

E. Dishevel, as in hair

__ __ __ __ __ __
26 46 59 63 78 76

F. Paired with corn or clam

__ __ __ __ __ __ __
3 72 65 75 54 16 29

G. Disfiguration

__ __ __ __ __ __ __ __ __
17 39 47 48 68 51 21 18 61

H. Education fee

__ __ __ __ __ __ __
64 49 31 74 70 19 15

I. Woodrow or Jackie

__ __ __ __ __ __
5 42 30 43 55 69

L. Affront

__ __ __ __ __ __
52 53 71 25 77 37

Answers on page 188.

Digital Sudoku

LOGIC

Use deductive logic to complete the grid so that each row, each column, and each 3 by 2 box contains the numbers 1 through 6 in some order. Some segments have been filled in. The solution is unique.

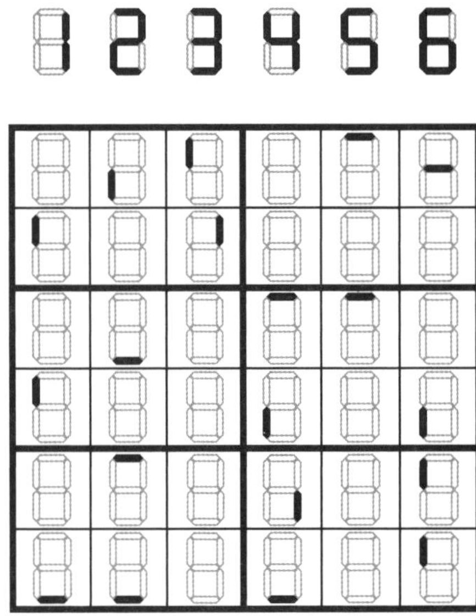

Marbles

ANALYSIS PLANNING

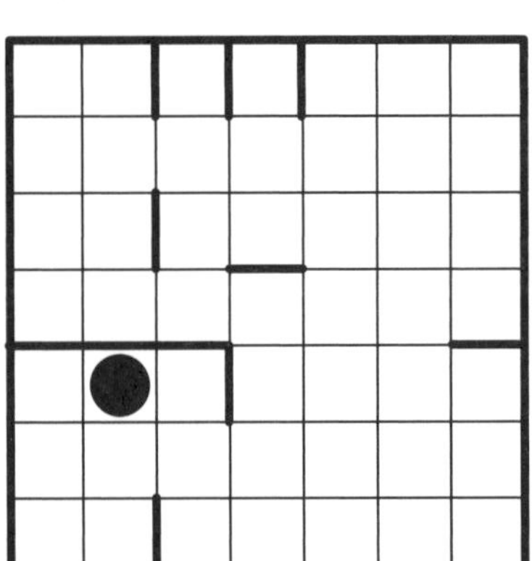

Place 12 marbles into the grid without having any touch one another, not even diagonally. There are some walls, represented by thick lines, that block the view of the marbles. Marbles must not "see" each other in a horizontal or vertical direction. We've placed the first 1 to get you started.

Answers on page 189.

Plan Ahead (Part I)

MEMORY

The following schedule is an excerpt from a planner for 12 days in the month of May. Study it for 5 minutes, then turn the page for a few memory-challenging questions.

Date	Morning	Afternoon	Evening
Monday 10		Dental appointment 2:30	
Tuesday 11	Business appointment with Cheesy Corporation 11:30		
Wednesday 12		Phone Dave	
Thursday 13			
Friday 14	Sales conference 8:30		Dinner with Kate and Tony 9:30
Saturday 15		Bowling 1:30	
Sunday 16			
Monday 17		Pick up Helena from airport 4:15	
Tuesday 18			
Wednesday 19	Mom and Dad's 35th Wedding Anniversary		
Thursday 20		Take car into garage for servicing 12:30	
Friday 21			

Plan Ahead (Part II)

MEMORY

(Do not read this until you've read the previous page!)

1. The planner covers 12 days during which month?
2. What wedding anniversary will be celebrated on Wednesday the 19th?
3. What time is the dental appointment on Monday?
4. With whom is the dinner date on Friday?
5. What appointment is scheduled for Tuesday the 11th?

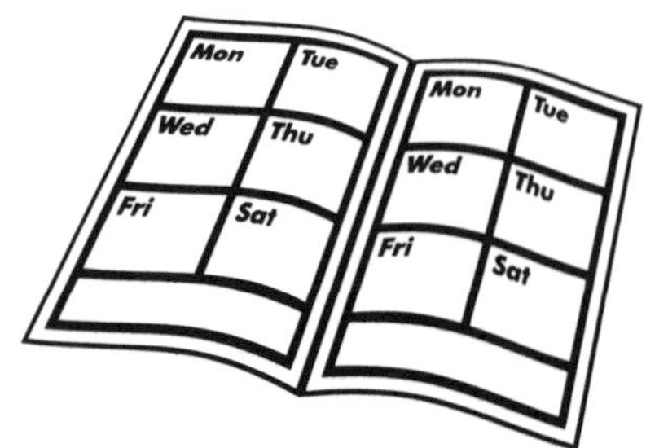

6. When is the car due to be taken in for servicing?
7. What other event occurs on the same day as the dinner date?
8. Who is scheduled to be picked up from the airport on Monday, and at what time?
9. What is scheduled for 1:30 on Saturday?
10. Who must be phoned in the afternoon on Wednesday the 12th?

Say What?

CREATIVE THINKING | LANGUAGE

Below are a group of words that, when properly arranged in the blanks, reveal a quote from a Ralph Waldo Emerson.

heard Always high young to what counsel are I do given

"It was ________ ________ that ________ had once ________ ________ ________ a ________ person, '________ do ________ you ________ afraid to ________.'"

Answers on page 189.

Word Columns

LANGUAGE PLANNING

Find the hidden quote from Bat Masterson by using the letters directly below each of the blank squares. Each letter is used only once. A black square or the end of the row indicates the end of a word.

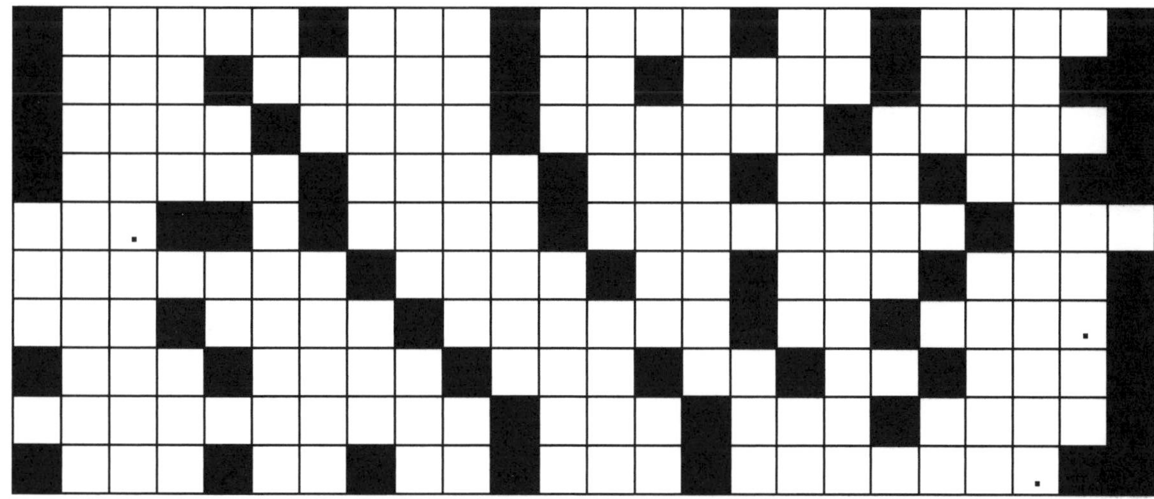

```
  x
  h o     t     a n     h       i f     o e
  h h e   r   c v e   m h b y   h n     o f
  o h e   r o r a h   t f n r   o s   p r o
  g e m d i e h m a   e n o s u r l n w h i k
  u e o u e t e h d e a f n n t r e t e e f o
t s b d r a t i i v m o o d o t a l b i t e t
s T l l e i i a r e g t t i e w i i l r c o e
e a a t s w m e l t a t a w i g a v l d h h s
u T m m p i t h t e n o u e t e s n e t g a r r
```

Answer on page 189.

Alien Mutations

PLANNING VISUAL LOGIC

Shown are 16 mutation chambers surrounded by alien figures. Each of the 4 aliens on the left passed through the 4 chambers to their right and transformed into the figure on the other side (e.g. the alien on the left of A passed through chambers A, B, C, and D and mutated into the alien to the right of D). The same is true for the aliens above the chambers: Each passed through the 4 chambers directly below them and came out mutated on the other side.

Each chamber affects 1—and only 1—alteration (changes in head or body shape, changes in posture, addition/removal of appendages). Note: Some chambers in the same row or column will undo what a previous chamber has done.

What mutation is each chamber responsible for?

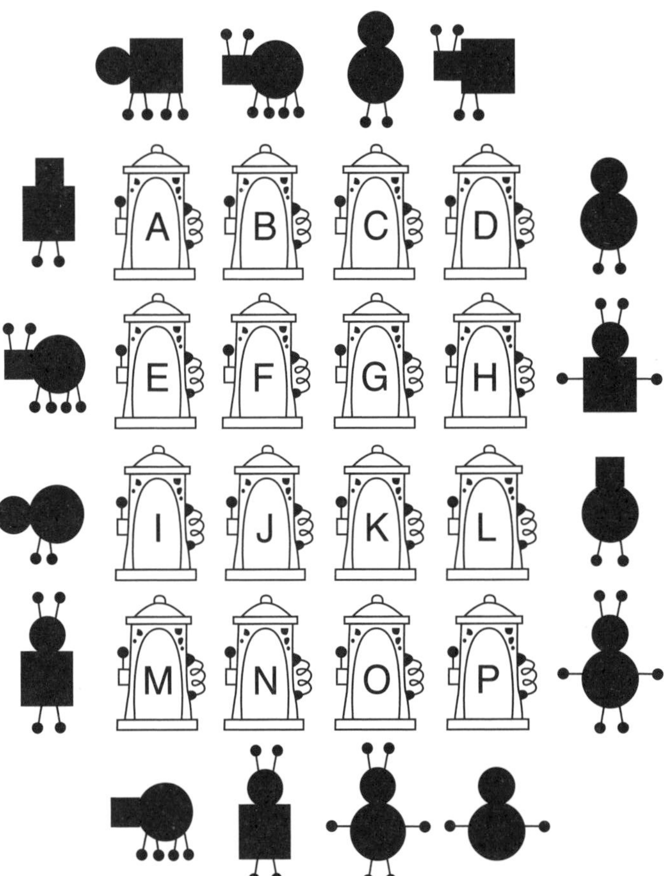

Answers on page 189.

Battle Boats

ANALYSIS LOGIC

Place each ship in the fleet located at right within the grid. Ships may be placed horizontally or vertically, but they don't touch each other, not even diagonally. Numbers reveal the ship segments located in that row or column.

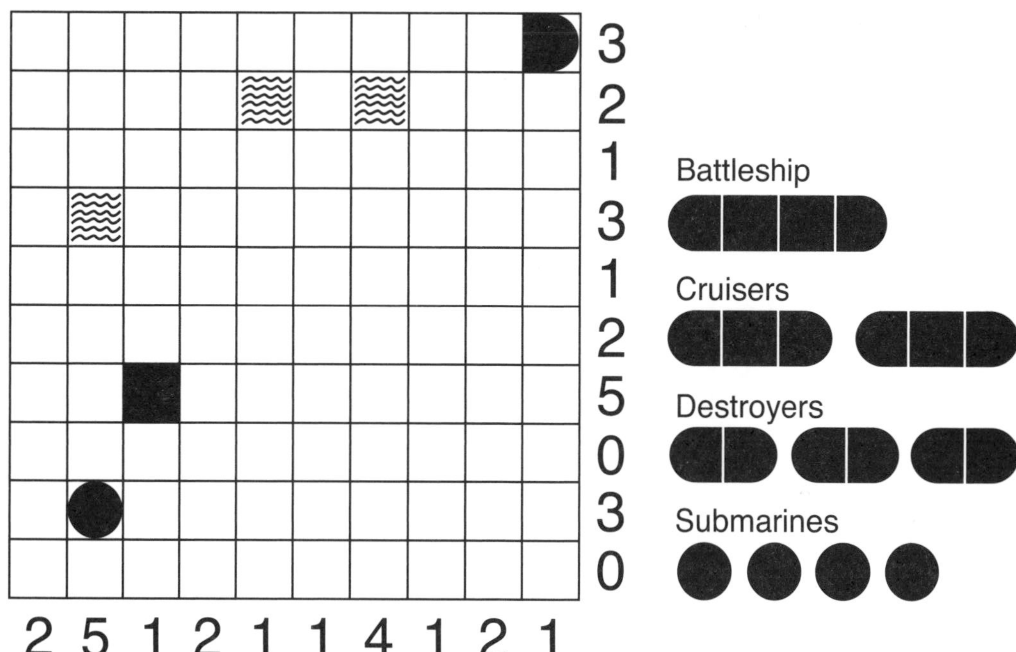

Trivia on the Brain

All of your "thoughts" are actually just a combination of electricity and chemicals in your brain.

Answer on page 189.

Red, White, Blue, and Green

CREATIVE THINKING | LOGIC

Two reds, 2 whites, 2 blues, and 2 greens are to be placed in every row, column, and long diagonal. The clues below will help you place them.

	A	B	C	D	E	F	G	H
1								
2								
3								
4								
5								
6								
7								
8								

1. Two greens, 2 whites, and a blue are directly enclosed by both the reds.
2. The greens are separated by 6 cells; there are no reds in cells E, F, G, or H.
3. The blues are separated by 6 cells; each green is immediately left of each red.
4. Each red is immediately left of each white.
5. No clue given.
6. Each white is immediately left of each blue.
7. A green and a red are directly enclosed by both the blues.
8. A blue and a white are directly enclosed by both the reds; the greens are not adjacent.

A. Two reds, a white, and a blue are directly enclosed by both the greens.
B. The reds are separated by 6 cells; the blues are adjacent.
C. The reds are adjacent.
D. Each red is immediately above each white.
E. Both the greens are directly enclosed by both the whites.
F. Both the reds are directly enclosed by both the blues.
G. No clue given.
H. Two blues, 2 whites, and a red are directly enclosed by both the greens.

Answer on page 189.

Cross Sums

COMPUTATION PLANNING

Use the numbers below to fill in the grid. Each cell at the top of a cross is the sum of numbers below it. So, as seen in the example, A=B+C+D+E.

1 2 4 5 6 7 8 10 11 12

17 29 34 38 69 80 118

280 296 301 995

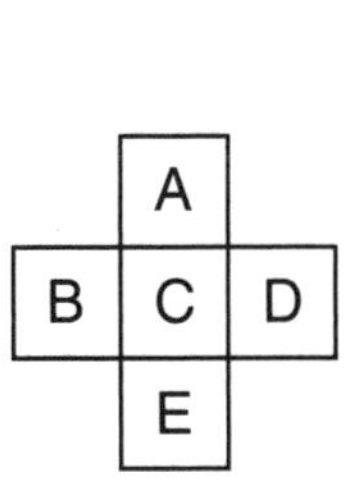

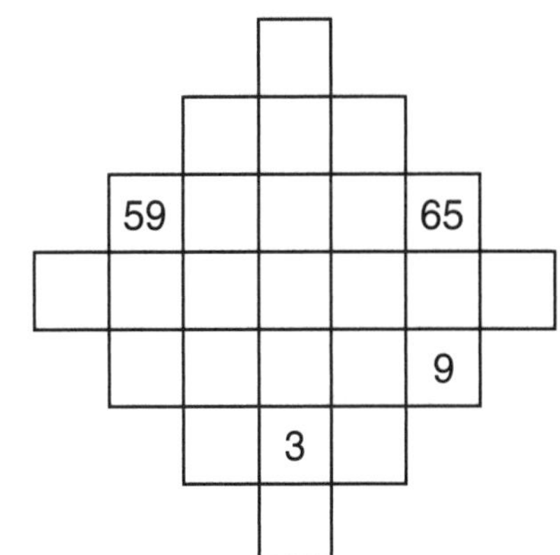

Crypto-Logic

COMPUTATION LOGIC

Each of the numbers in the sequence below represents a letter. Use the mathematical clues to determine which number stands for which letter and reveal the encrypted word.

5 3 2 5 9 6 1

Clues:

2A + 2U = X

2N = X

X = 3A + U + D

E = U + A + D

C + D = X

E = 6

Answers on pages 189–190.

Mastermind

LOGIC

5	3	9	1	0	● ○ ○
8	0	4	6	5	● ○ ○
1	4	9	2	7	● ○ ○
6	9	2	7	4	● ○ ○
7	5	0	3	8	● ○ ○
?	0	?	5	?	

Determine the correct order of the numbers below with the help of the indicators given in each row. A black dot means that a number is in the correct position in that row; a white dot means the correct number is in that row, but in the wrong position. Digits do not appear more than once in the solution, and the solution never begins with 0.

Window Boxes

ANALYSIS LOGIC

There's a pattern to this skyline. Can you discover what it is and correctly fill in the 2 missing windows in this view of downtown Toronto?

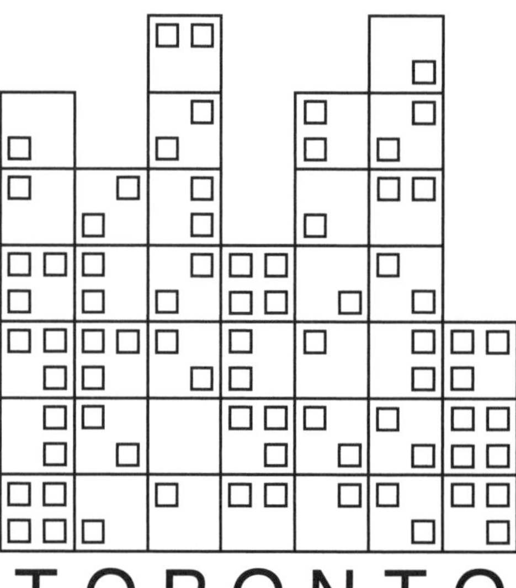

Answers on page 190.

Snake Shapes

CREATIVE THINKING | SPATIAL VISUALIZATION | VISUAL LOGIC

Which of the 3 shapes below fit into the grid without overlapping its borders? Shapes may be rotated but not mirrored.

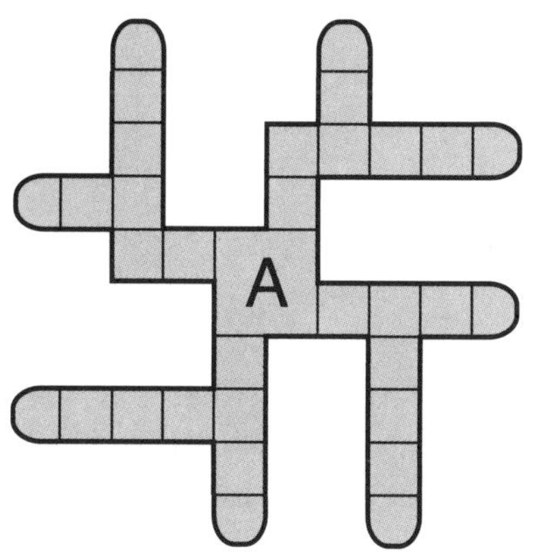

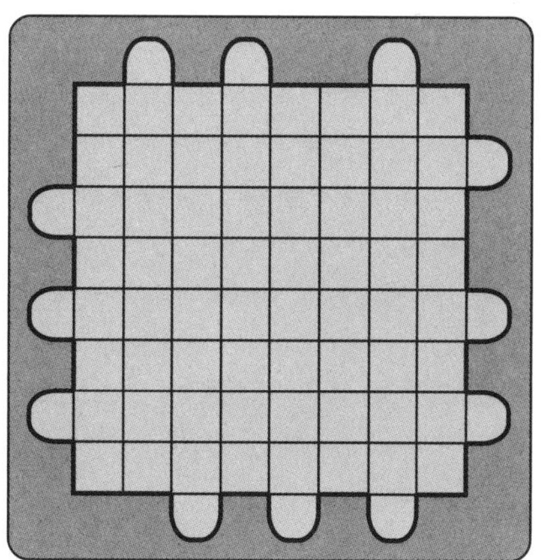

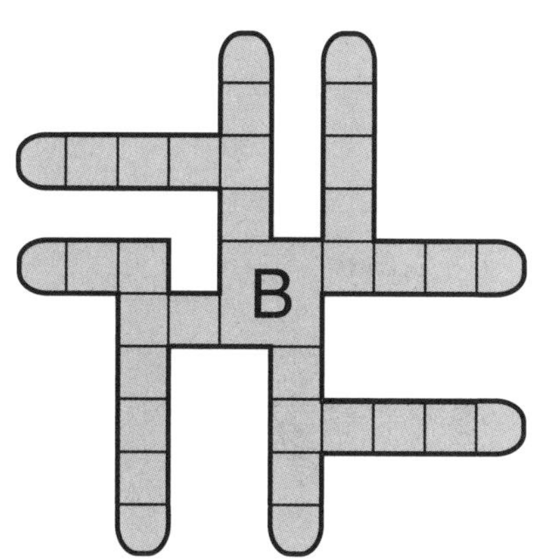

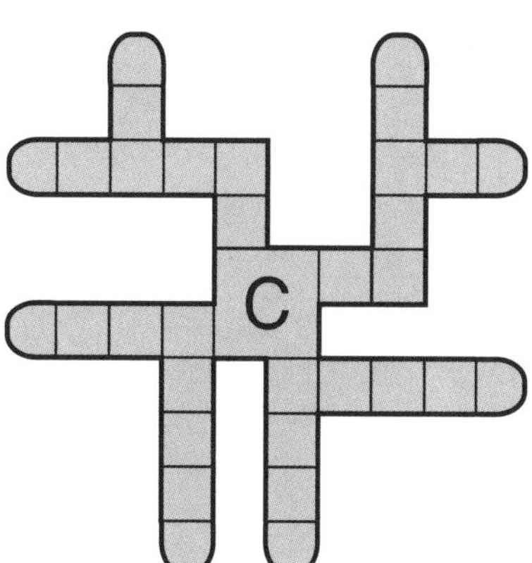

Answer on page 190.

REASSESS YOUR BRAIN

You have just completed a set of puzzles selected to challenge your various mental skills. We hope you enjoyed them. And did the mental exercise you engaged in also improve your memory, attention, problem-solving, and other important cognitive skills? In order to find out, please fill out this questionnaire. It is the same one you filled out before you embarked on our puzzles. So now you will be in a position to compare your cognitive skills before and after you challenged them with cognitive exercise. The real question is whether solving our puzzles had a real impact on your real-life performance. We hope it did.

The questions below are designed to test your skills in the areas of memory, problem-solving, creative thinking, attention, language, and more. Please take a moment to think about your answers and rate your responses on a 5-point scale, where 5 equals "excellent" and 1 equals "very poor." Then tally up your scores, and go to the categories at the bottom of the next page to see how you did.

1. You get a new cell phone. How long does it take you to remember the number? Give yourself a 1 if you have to check the phone every time you want to give out the number and a 5 if you know it by heart the next day.

   1 2 3 4 5

2. How good are you at remembering where you put things? Give yourself a 5 if you never lose anything but a 1 if you have to search for the keys every time you want to leave the house.

   1 2 3 4 5

3. You have a busy work day that you've carefully planned around a doctor's appointment. At the last minute, the doctor's office calls and asks you to reschedule your appointment from afternoon to morning. How good are you at juggling your plans to accommodate this change?

   1 2 3 4 5

4. You're taking a trip back to your hometown and have several old friends to see, as well as old haunts to visit. You'll only be there for three days. How good are you at planning your visit so you can accomplish everything?

   1 2 3 4 5

5. A friend takes you to a movie, and the next morning a curious coworker wants to hear the plot in depth. How good are you at remembering all the details?

   1 2 3 4 5

6. Consider this scenario: You're brokering an agreement between two parties (could be anything from a business merger to making peace between feuding siblings), and both parties keep changing their demands. How good are you at adapting to the changing situation?

   1 2 3 4 5

7. You're cooking a big meal for a family celebration. Say you have to cook everything—appetizers, entrees, sides, and desserts—all on the same day. How good are you at planning out each recipe so that everything is done and you can sit down and enjoy the meal with your family?

   1 2 3 4 5

8. In an emotionally charged situation (for example, when you're giving a toast), can you usually come up with the right words to describe your feelings?

   1 2 3 4 5

9. You and five friends have made a vow to always spend a certain amount of money on each other for holiday gifts. How good are you at calculating the prices of things in your head to make sure you spend the right amount of money?

   1 2 3 4 5

10. You're moving, and you have to coordinate all the details of packing, hiring movers, cutting off and setting up utilities, and a hundred other small details. How good are you at planning out this complex situation?

    1 2 3 4 5

10–25 Points: Are You Ready to Make a Change?
Remember, it's never too late to improve your brain health! A great way to start is to work puzzles each day, and you've taken the first step by buying this book. Choose a different type of puzzle each day, or do a variety of them to help strengthen memory, focus, attention, and improve logic and problem-solving.

26–40 Points: Building Your Mental Muscle
You're no mental slouch, but there's always room to sharpen your mind! Choose puzzles that will challenge you, especially the types of puzzles you might not like as much or wouldn't normally do. Remember, doing a puzzle can be the mental equivalent of doing lunges or squats: While they might not be your first choice of activities, you'll definitely like the results!

41–50 Points: View from the Top
Congratulations! You're keeping your brain in tip-top shape. To maintain this level of mental fitness, keep challenging yourself by working puzzles every day. Like the rest of the body's muscles, your mental strength can decline if you don't use it. So choose to keep your brain supple and strong. You're at the summit, now you just have to stay to enjoy the view!

ANSWERS

ABCD (page 11)

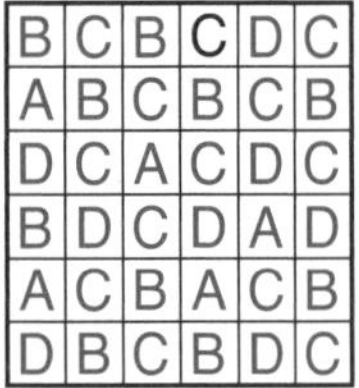

Spell Math! (page 11)

Three + seven = ten

Codeword (page 12)

Word-a-Maze: On the Go (page 13)

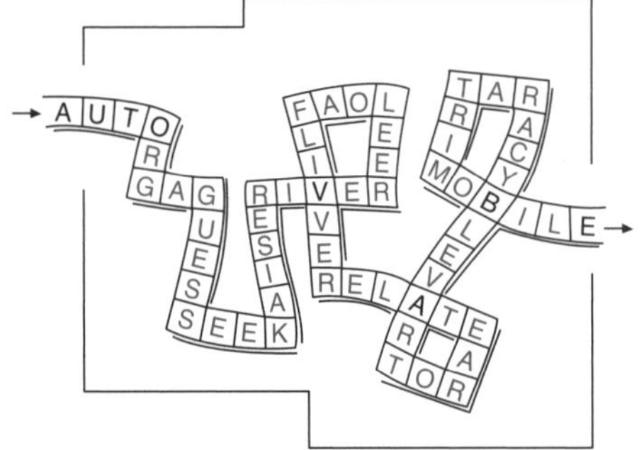

The "T" Sound (page 14)

The leftover letters spell: T is for the tears she shed to save me.

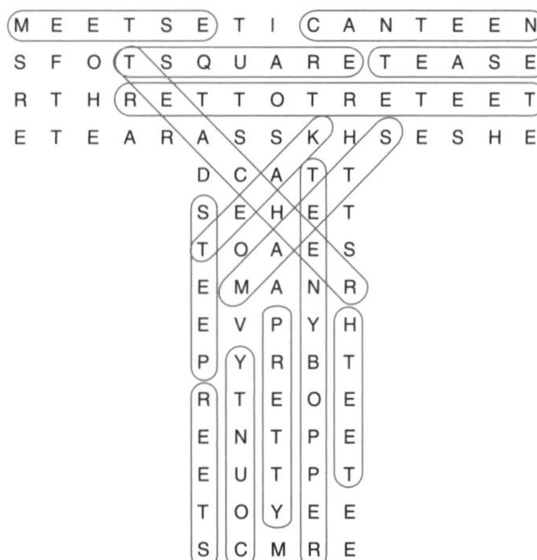

Battle Boats (page 15)

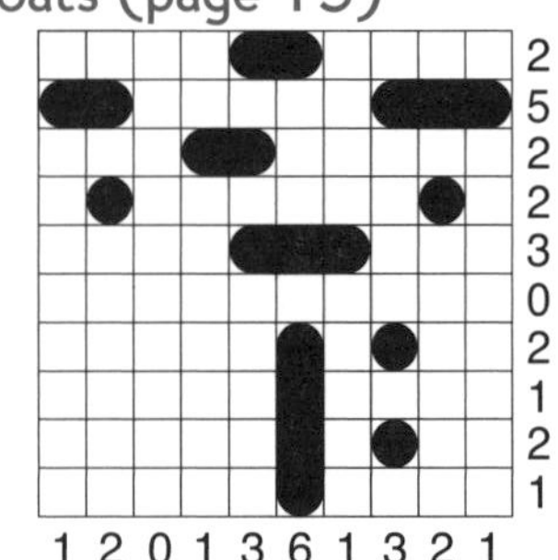

Famous Anagrams (page 15)

A. Donald Duck; B. Mickey Mouse;
C. RUPERT MURDOCH; D. Bugs Bunny

It's Magic! (pages 16–17)

1-2-3 (page 18)

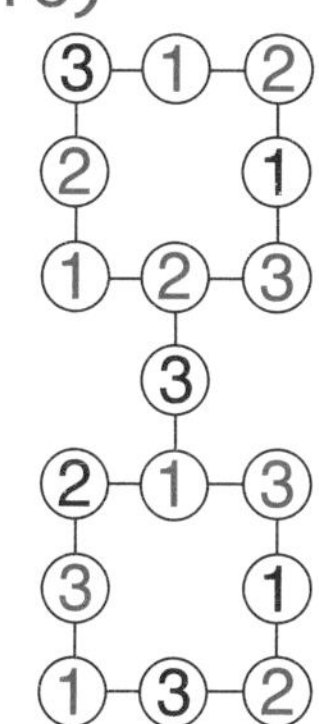

Crypto-Logic (page 18)

NEAT. If S is 5, I is 10. If I is 10, T is 1. Therefore N is 4. 4 – A = 1, so A is 3. Therefore E is 9.

Try Your Luck (page 19)

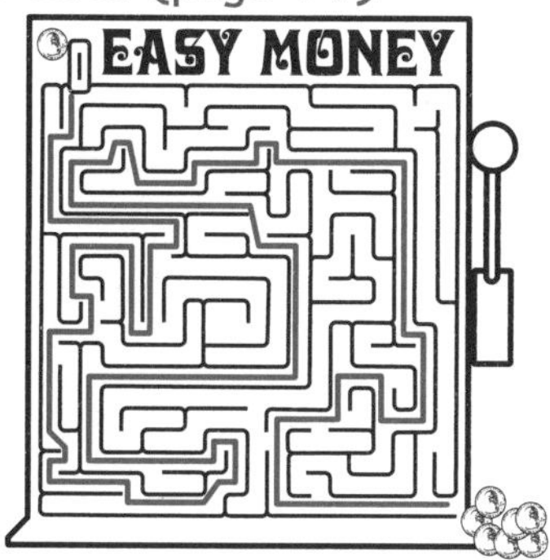

Say What? (page 19)

"A dirty joke is a sort of mental rebellion."

—George Orwell

Shenanigans (page 20)

MOON – O + KEY + BUS + LINES – L + S = MONKEY BUSINESS

Fitting Words (page 20)

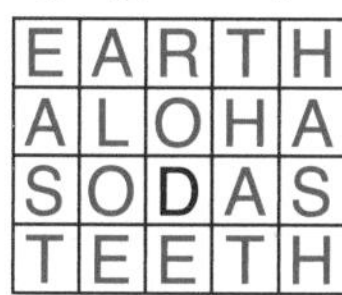

E	A	R	T	H
A	L	O	H	A
S	O	D	A	S
T	E	E	T	H

Ring-Around-a-Rosie (page 21)

L'adder (page 22)

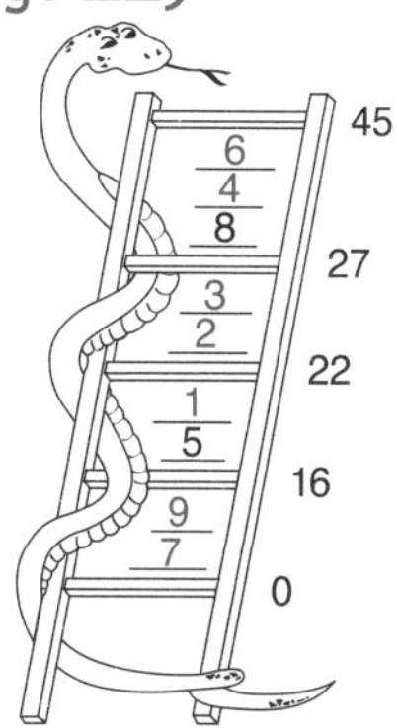

Dissection (page 22)

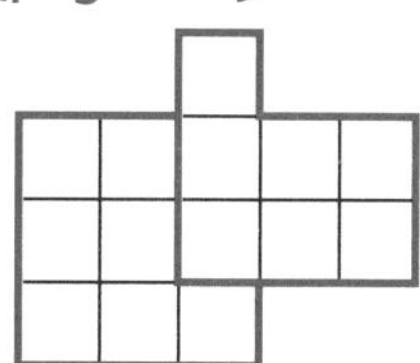

Word Ladder (page 23)

BALL, pall, pail, pain, pawn, YAWN

Code-doku (page 23)

F	K	I	P	C	S	N	E	R
S	E	P	R	I	N	K	C	F
C	N	R	E	K	F	I	P	S
R	I	C	S	F	E	P	K	N
E	P	S	K	N	R	F	I	C
N	F	K	I	P	C	S	R	E
P	R	E	F	S	I	C	N	K
K	C	F	N	R	P	E	S	I
I	S	N	C	E	K	R	F	P

FINE PRINCE KISSES PRINCESS

Answers

Bee-Bop Jive (page 24)

Elevator Words (page 25)

1. JUMBO jet; 2. jet ski; 3. ski tow; 4. tow truck; 5. truck stop; 6. stop sign; 7. sign LANGUAGE

Vex-a-Gon (page 25)

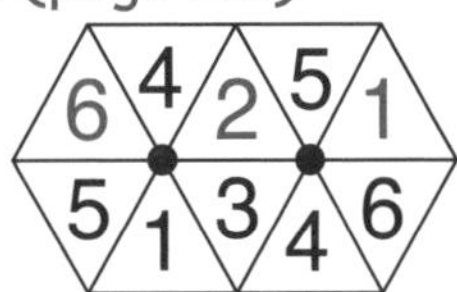

Crossed Words (page 26)

Chalk, cheese

Cross Sums (page 26)

			101			
		40	33	28		
	14	15	11	7	10	
3	6	5	4	2	1	7

Hashi (page 27)

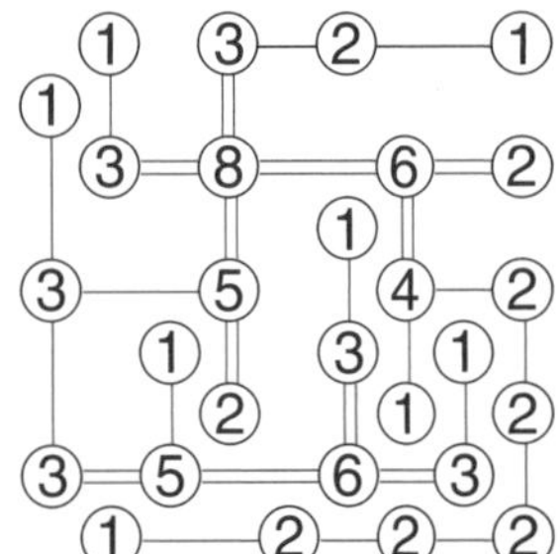

We, the Jury by Alpha Sleuth™ (page 28)

COURT JESTER

Calcu-doku (page 29)

4	3	1	2
3	2	4	1
1	4	2	3
2	1	3	4

Arrow Web (page 29)

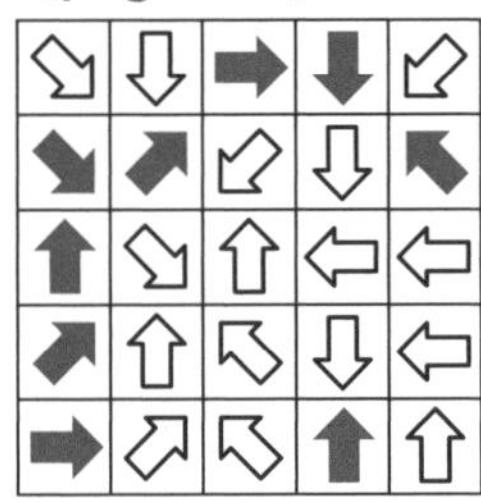

XOXO (page 30)

Answers may vary.

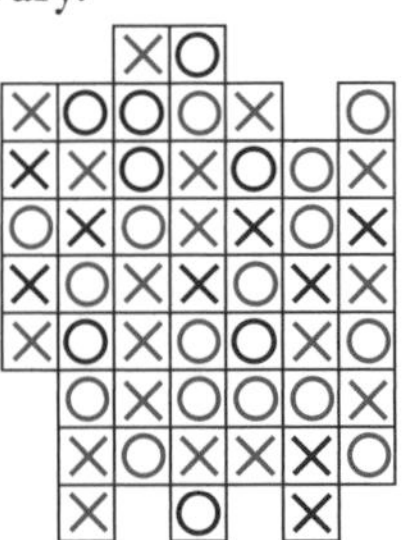

Word Jigsaw (page 30)

Name Calling (page 31)

Laughing stock—cattle with a sense of humor.

Cluster (page 31)

Short Sequence (page 32)

S (Clubs, Diamonds, Hearts, Spades)

Fit It (pages 32–33)

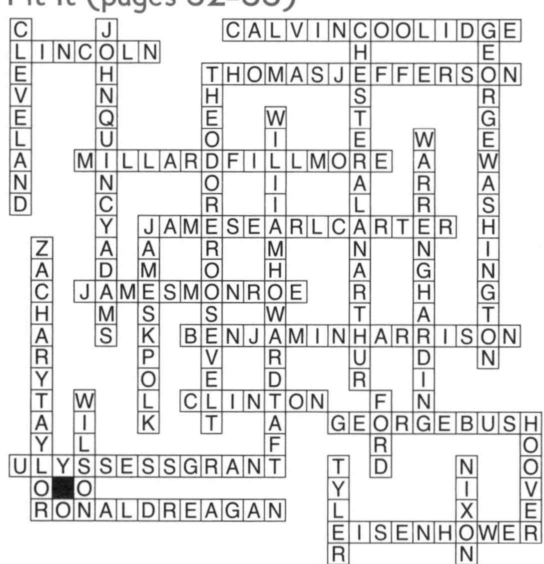

Star Power (page 34)

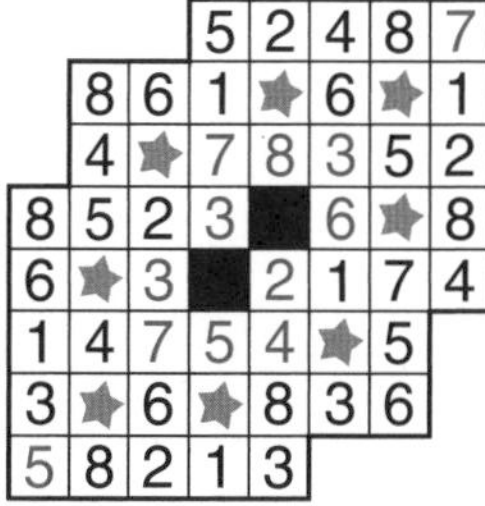

Cross-Math (page 35)

7	-	6	+	8	=	9
+		+		-		
1	+	5	×	3	=	18
+		+		-		
9	+	4	×	2	=	26
=		=		=		
17		15		3		

Word Ladder (page 35)

KETTLE, mettle, nettle, nestle, PESTLE

Rhyme Time (page 36)

1. got hot; 2. Cub snub; 3. slow flow; 4. dorm form; 5. finer liner; 6. rift shift; 7. muddy study; 8. reach beach; 9. stock shock; 10. regal eagle

Kakuro (page 37)

Network (page 37)

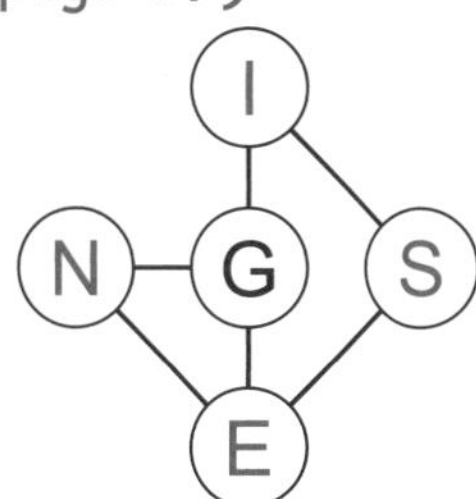

GENESIS

Answers

Code-doku (page 38)

EDINBURGH

Perfect Score (page 38)

50 + 41 + 9 = 100

Monetary Scramblegram (page 39)

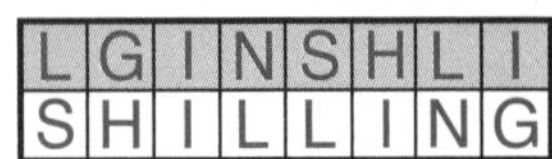

Eavesdropping Logic (page 40)

The answer is D. We can't establish B or C (although C may be implied, it can not be deduced from the situation as described).

Missing Connections (page 40)

Fences (page 41)

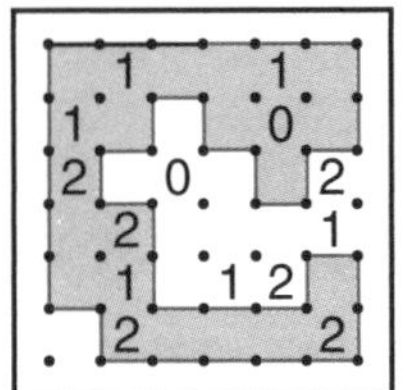

Twenty-four Jumble (page 41)

$5 \times 4 + 4 = 24$

Black Diamonds (page 42)

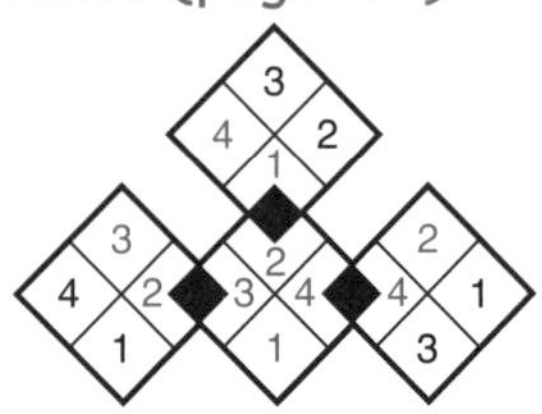

Marbles (page 42)

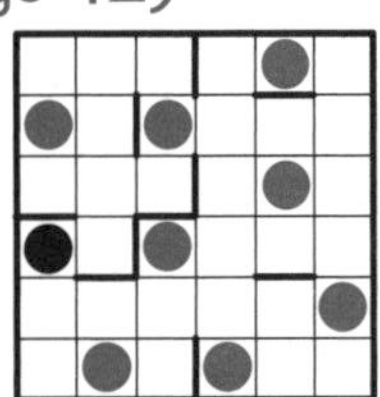

May the Force Be With You (page 43)

Leftover letters spell: "He's quite clever, you know... for a human being."

L'adder (page 44)

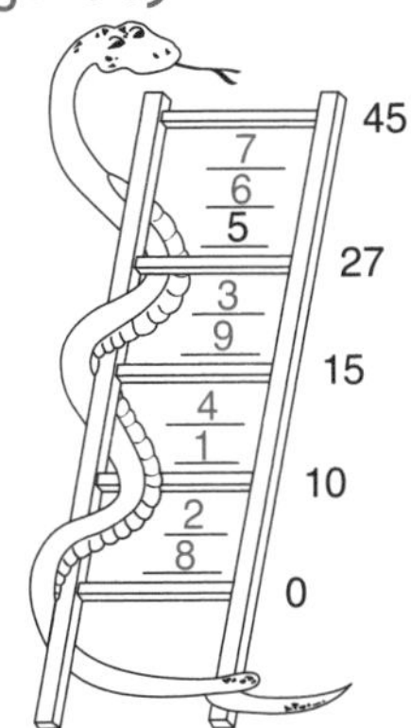

A Puzzling Perspective (page 44)

ATMOSPHERIC

Fitting Words (page 45)

O	C	C	U	R
H	O	U	S	E
M	I	R	E	D
S	L	E	D	S

Calcu-doku (page 45)

4	2	3	1
1	4	2	3
2	3	1	4
3	1	4	2

Flip the Cards (page 46)

C. One doesn't need to ensure that all cards with a 5 have an R on the reverse, nor that every G has a 6. But one does need to check the 6 and see if it has a G on the back.

Word Jigsaw (page 46)

Alien Mutations (page 47)

A remove rear appendages; B head square; C add antennae; D head circle; E to quadruped; F add front appendages; G add front appendages; H remove antennae; I to biped

Seafood Dinner Date (pages 48–49)

Pampered Pups (page 50)

1. groomer's hair now dark; 2. hearts on uniform; 3. bottle missing; 4. shelves have no sides; 5. clock has different time; 6. picture changed; 7. pocket on uniform missing; 8. bow vanished; 9. bone placed on dog bed; 10. no food in dish; 11. wearing a glove; 12. door gone from cabinet; 13. dog's tongue out; 14. brush changed position

Vex-a-Gon (page 51)

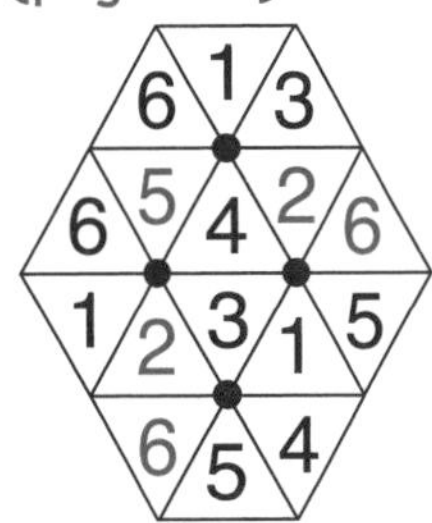

Name Calling (page 51)

One good deed has many claimants.

Answers

Clapboard (pages 52–53)

B	A	R	B	E	R	E	M	O	T	E	B	B
A	V	E	R	T	A	R	O	T	I	G	E	R
R	E	C	O	U	P	R	O	O	F	O	R	E
B	R	O	W	I	S	E	R	E	F	U	T	E
R	A	I	N	S	O	D	A	R	E	S	O	D
O	G	L	E	L	I	O	T	E	N	T	R	U
A	R	I	D	E	L	T	A	D	D	I	N	G
D	I	V	E	P	E	E	S	E	E	P	A	R
A	P	E	N	T	E	N	S	E	R	O	D	E
S	E	N	O	R	S	O	A	R	O	T	O	E
A	W	E	D	E	T	R	O	I	T	A	L	K
L	O	S	E	R	O	Y	A	L	O	T	E	E
T	O	T	S	A	P	E	T	E	R	O	O	D

Clone It! (page 54)

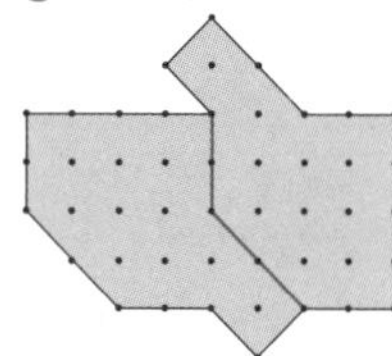

Cast-a-Word (page 54)

1. A F H I K W; 2. B M O P T Z;
3. C L N R S U; 4. D E G J Q Y

Team Search (page 55)

Leftover letters spell: "A team is where a boy can prove his courage on his own. A gang is where a coward goes to hide."

Bonus answer: Diamondbacks

Perfect Score (page 56)

1 + 30 + 69 = 100

Crypto-Group: Comic Book Heroes (page 56)

Batman; Daredevil; Black Widow; Iron Fist; Cyclops

Quic-Kross (page 57)

B	O	A	T
G	R	A	M
H	E	A	T
H	A	N	G

G	S	M	T
R	A	A	A
I	N	R	R
T	D	T	T

Word Ladder (page 57)

GRATE, irate, crate, crane, crone, DRONE

Naughty Students (page 58)

	Name	Surname	Crime	Punishment
1	Andy	Finkel	stealing books	forfeiting sport
2	Colin	Harrow	eating in class	cleaning windows
3	Denzil	Goof	talking back	mopping floors
4	Bernard	Everong	breaking chairs	extra assignments

ABCD (page 59)

A	B	C	A	C	B
B	A	B	D	B	D
C	B	D	A	D	A
D	C	B	D	C	B
A	B	A	C	D	A
C	D	C	A	C	D

Calcu-doku (page 59)

3	4	2	1
4	1	3	2
2	3	1	4
1	2	4	3

Elevator Words (page 60)

1. KNOW how; 2. how come; 3. come clean; 4. clean hands; 5. hands off; 6. off base; 7. base HIT

Fences (page 60)

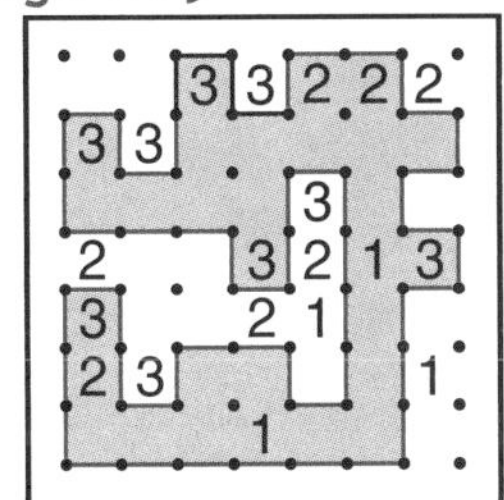

What's Flipped in Vegas, Stays in Vegas (page 61)

The coin came up heads 12 times.

Sudoku (page 61)

2	3	9	6	7	1	4	8	5
8	1	6	2	5	4	9	7	3
5	4	7	8	3	9	2	1	6
1	2	4	9	6	5	7	3	8
6	7	5	3	8	2	1	9	4
9	8	3	4	1	7	6	5	2
4	6	1	5	9	3	8	2	7
7	5	2	1	4	8	3	6	9
3	9	8	7	2	6	5	4	1

Spell Math! (page 62)

Six + nine = fifteen

Fit It (pages 62–63)

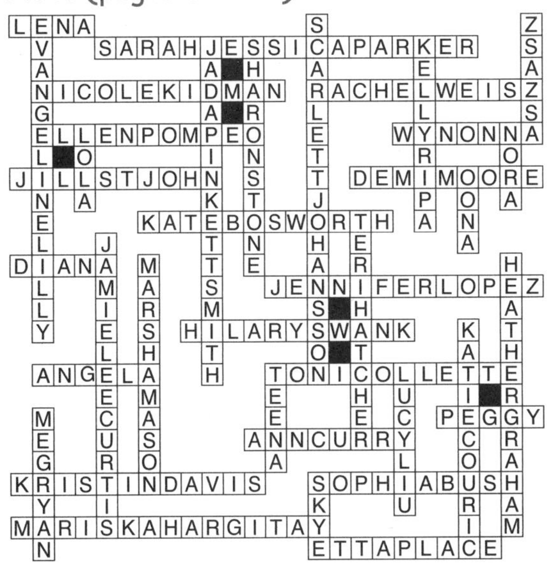

Retro Rocket Maze (page 64)

Word-a-Maze: Measured (page 65)

Star Power (page 66)

			8	1	3	2	4
	5	3	4	★	6	★	5
	1	★	2	5	7	8	1
5	8	7	6	■	4	★	3
3	★	2	■	3	5	6	2
6	4	1	8	4	★	8	
5	★	3	★	2	1	7	
8	2	7	5	6			

Answers

1-2-3 (page 67)

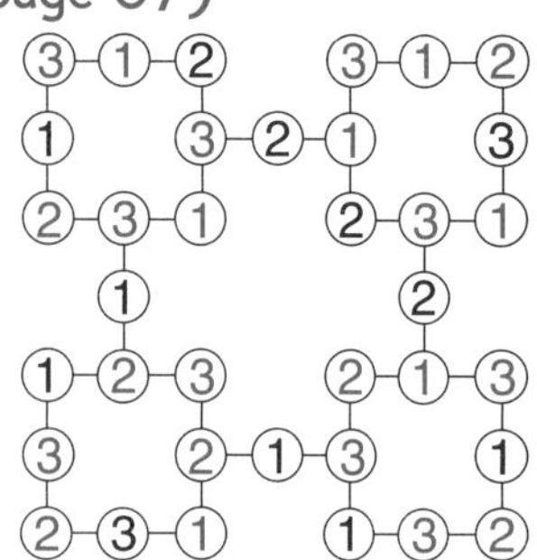

Word Ladder (page 67)

SLEEP, sleet, slept, swept, sweet, SKEET

Word Columns (page 68)

"The great proof of madness is the disproportion of one's designs to one's means."

Minesweeper (page 68)

3	*		1			1	*		1
*	*	2		*	1		1		*
3				2					1
1	*	2	1		*	1			
		*				1	1	*	
		1		1				2	*
*			1	1	*	1		1	1
2		*	2						
*		1		*	*	1		*	*
1			1		2	1		*	3

Cross Count (page 69)

7 p	1 a	9 r	17
5 e	9 r	1 a	15
2 t	5 e	5 n	12
14	15	15	

Double Jumble (page 69)

M	DILEMMA	T
O	MARTINI	R
D	ELEGANT	A
E	OCTAGON	I
L	LEATHER	N

Animal House? (page 70)

"I realized I was dyslexic when I went to a toga party dressed as a goat."

—Comedian Marcus Brigstocke

Kakuro (page 70)

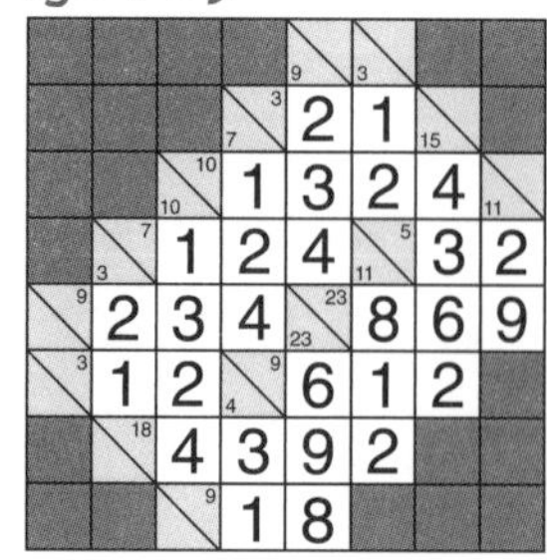

Hitori (page 71)

1	**5**	3	5	8	**1**	2	**8**
2	5	8	3	**5**	6	1	4
5	**5**	4	7	6	1	8	2
6	7	5	1	**3**	3	**3**	8
3	8	2	6	1	5	4	**4**
4	**5**	6	**1**	3	**3**	5	7
2	4	1	2	5	7	**1**	6
8	1	7	**3**	2	**5**	6	3

Spell Math! (page 71)

Four + nine = thirteen

Missing Connections (page 72)

Word Jigsaw (page 72)

Uncrossed Paths (page 73)

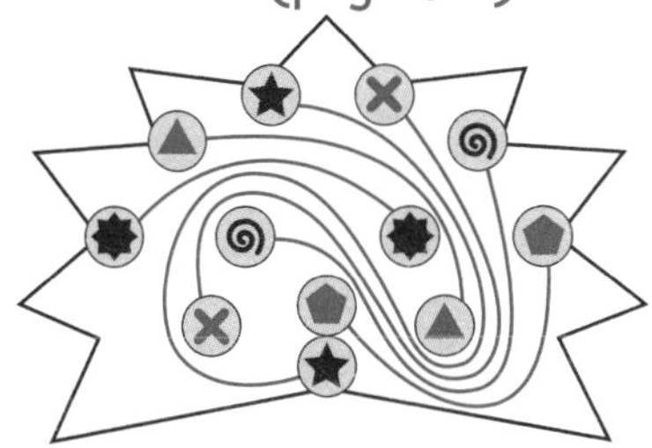

Sudoku (page 74)

4	7	3	2	6	9	1	8	5
2	5	8	1	4	7	6	9	3
9	6	1	8	5	3	7	2	4
3	4	2	6	7	8	5	1	9
5	8	9	3	1	4	2	6	7
7	1	6	9	2	5	4	3	8
8	2	7	5	9	1	3	4	6
1	9	4	7	3	6	8	5	2
6	3	5	4	8	2	9	7	1

Eavesdropping Logic (page 74)

The answer is C, as it is not obvious that anyone is being negative, and Belinda being lonely is a misreading of the term "alone" in the passage.

Elevator Words (page 75)

1. ADAM'S apple; 2. apple tree; 3. tree snake; 4. snake oil; 5. oil spill; 6. spill way; 7. way TO GO

Vex-a-Gon (page 75)

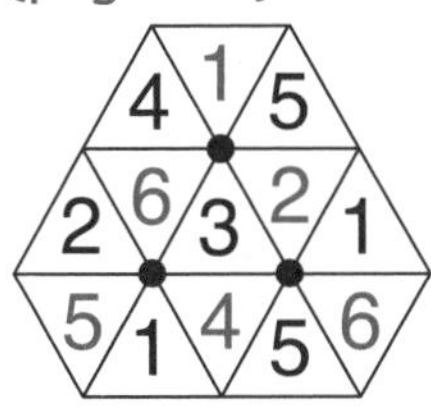

Scientific Discoveries (page 76)

	Name	Surname	Discovery
1	Michael	Darling	splitting apple
2	Charles	Friday	gravy tree
3	Albert	Bore	eccentricity
4	Isaac	Newtune	relative pity
5	Niels	Eyeline	devolution

Mastermind (page 76)

164

Diamond Mining (page 77)

Leftover letters spell: "Better a diamond with a flaw than a pebble without."

Grid Fill (page 78)

F	A	B	L	E
T	R	I	E	D
V	I	C	E	S
R	U	S	T	Y
H	A	Z	E	L
D	R	O	V	E

Rhyme Time (page 78)

1. wise guys; 2. dark park; 3. aching raking; 4. treason reason; 5. Esau's seesaws

Star Power (page 79)

6	5	4		1	2	5				
7	★	3	8	6	★	4	6	5		
8	1	2	★	7	8	3	★	2		
		1	4	5	★	1	8	7		
		6	★	2	4	6	★	2	3	7
		7	3	8	★	3	4	5	★	4
				1	5	7		6	1	8

Anagram Snack (page 80)

SPECTRUM/CRUMPETS

Answers

Odd-Even Logidoku (page 80)

3	6	7	5	2	4	1	9	8
4	1	5	7	9	8	3	6	2
8	9	2	1	3	6	5	4	7
9	3	8	6	7	2	4	5	1
5	2	6	9	4	1	8	7	3
7	4	1	3	8	5	9	2	6
6	8	9	2	5	3	7	1	4
2	7	3	4	1	9	6	8	5
1	5	4	8	6	7	2	3	9

Discovering America by Alpha Sleuth™ (page 81)

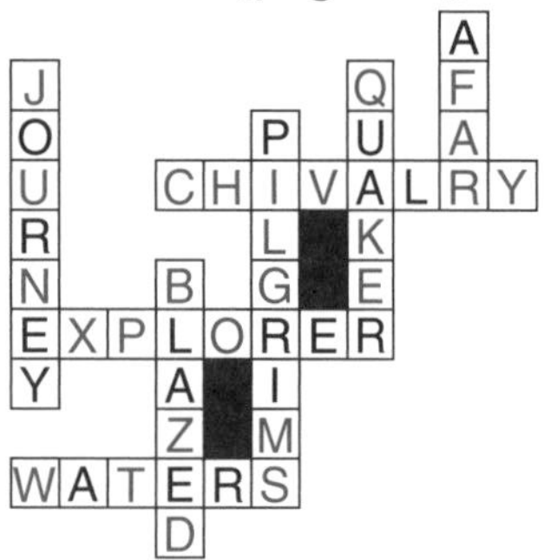

MAIDEN VOYAGE

Calcu-doku (page 82)

1	5	3	2	4
3	1	2	4	5
2	3	4	5	1
4	2	5	1	3
5	4	1	3	2

Fitting Words (page 82)

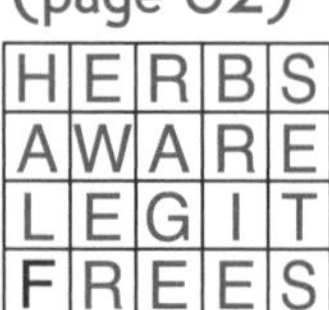

Battle Boats (page 83)

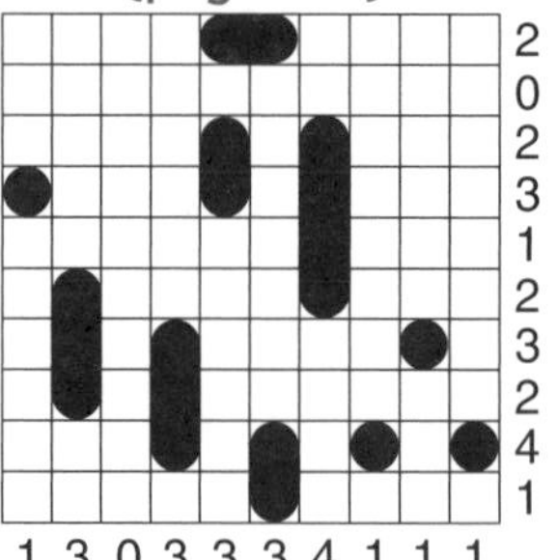

Current Events (pages 84–85)

Cross Sums (page 86)

426

160 143 123

54 55 51 37 35

15 18 21 16 14 7 14

3 5 7 6 8 2 4 1 9

Word Jigsaw (page 86)

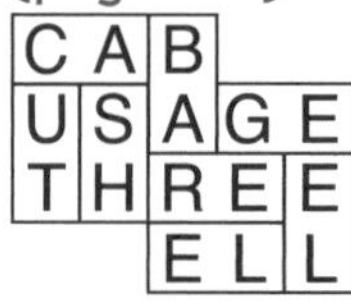

Missing Connections (page 87)

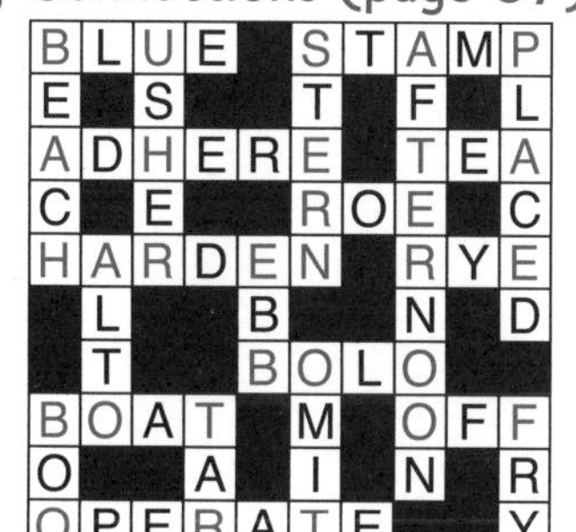

1-2-3 (page 88)

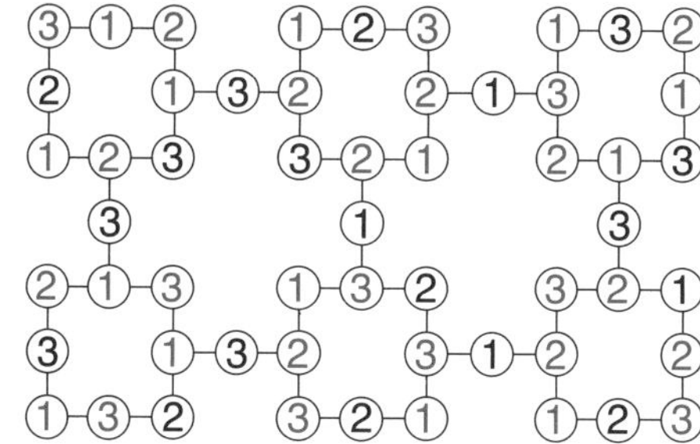

From A to Z (page 89)

Leftover letters spell: Glad to see you know your ABCs.

Alien Mutations (page 90)

A add antennae; B add front appendages; C remove rear appendages; D to quadruped; E remove antennae; F head circle; G head circle; H body circle; I body square; J body circle; K add antennae; L to biped

Twenty-four Jumble (page 91)

$5 \times 5 - 5 + 4 = 24$

Marbles (page 91)

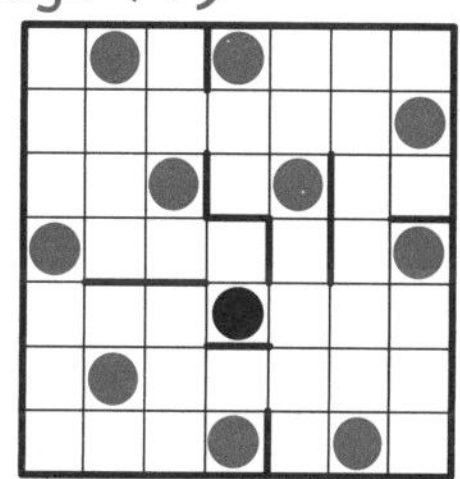

Get It Straight (page 92)

Code-doku (page 93)

T	H	J	L	N	Y	O	E	R
L	E	R	J	O	T	N	H	Y
O	Y	N	R	E	H	L	J	T
R	J	L	E	Y	O	H	T	N
Y	T	H	N	R	L	E	O	J
E	N	O	H	T	J	R	Y	L
N	L	Y	O	J	E	T	R	H
H	O	T	Y	L	R	J	N	E
J	R	E	T	H	N	Y	L	O

JOHN TYLER

Answers

L'adder (page 94)

Answers may vary.

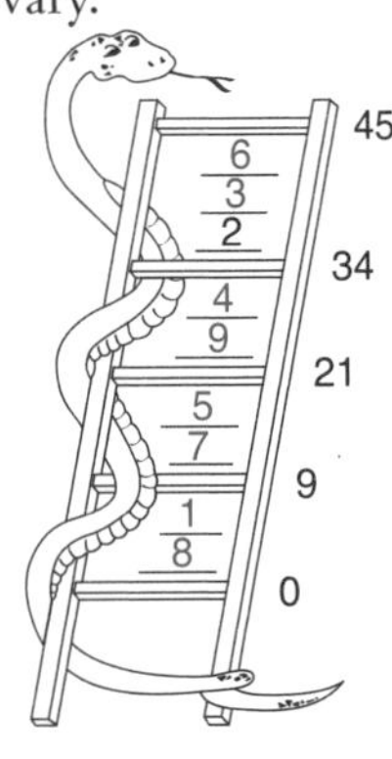

Cross Sums (page 94)

				279				
			87	84	108			
		38	25	24	35	49		
	19	12	7	6	11	18	20	
8	7	4	1	2	3	6	9	5

Hashi (page 95)

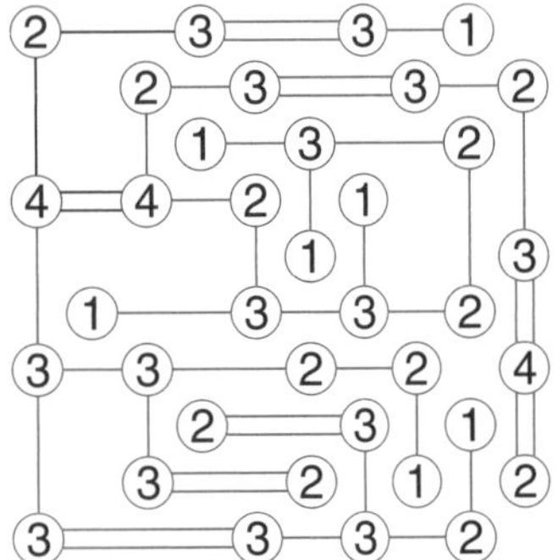

ABCD (page 96)

D	A	D	A	D	B
A	C	B	C	B	C
C	B	D	A	D	B
D	C	A	D	B	C
B	A	B	C	A	B
D	C	A	D	C	A

Flip the Cards (page 96)

A

Cross Count (page 97)

3 c	9 r	5 e	5 e	22
8 h	9 i	3 l	3 l	23
1 a	3 l	1 a	1 s	6
9 r	5 e	5 n	5 e	24
21	26	14	14	

Calcu-doku (page 97)

4	2	5	1	3
1	4	3	5	2
3	5	1	2	4
5	3	2	4	1
2	1	4	3	5

Word Columns (page 98)

"The one thing sure about politics is that what goes up comes down and what goes down often comes up." —Richard Nixon

Snake Shapes (page 99)

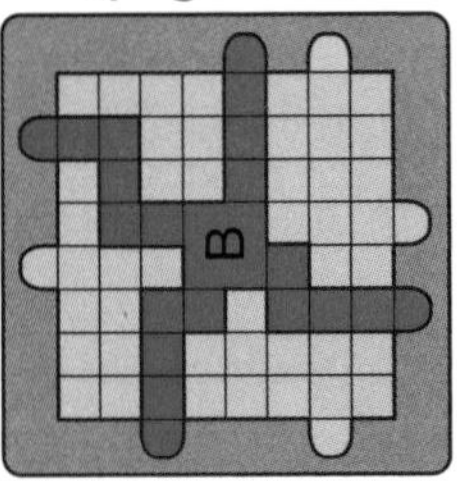

Cast-a-Word (page 99)

1. A H I M P S; 2. B E F G T Y; 3. C D L N Q V; 4. K O R U W X

Perfect Score (page 100)

92 + 4 + 4 = 100

Word Jigsaw (page 100)

Silly Proverbs (page 101)

	Adjective	Noun 1	Verb	Noun 2
1	fat	mice	eat	lipgloss
2	stinking	spiders	love	pizza
3	ugly	rhinos	need	fame
4	demented	cats	attack	mud
5	crazy	fleas	avoid	crowds

Kakuro (page 102)

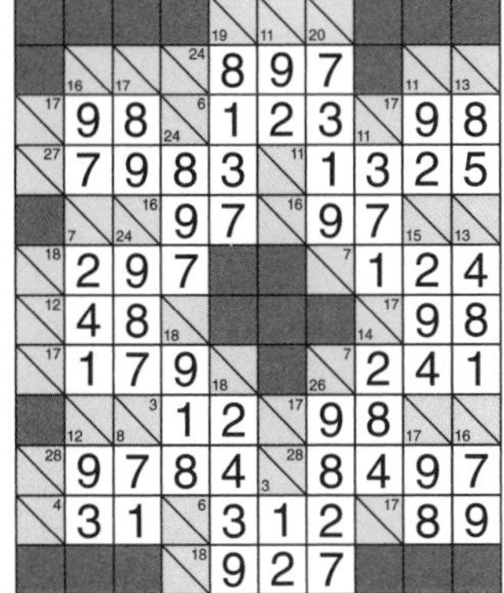

Identity Parade (page 103)

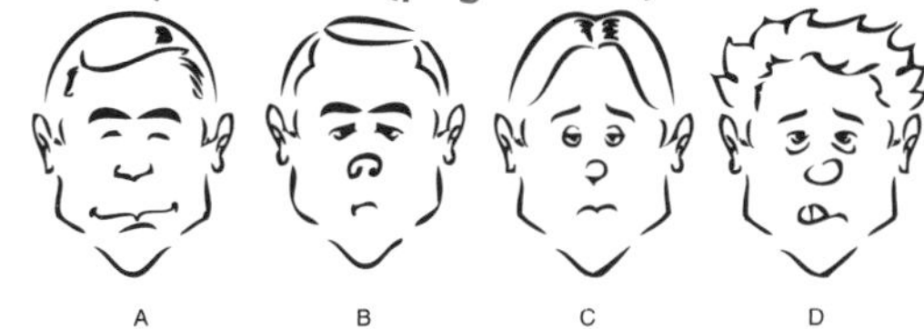

Digital Sudoku (page 104)

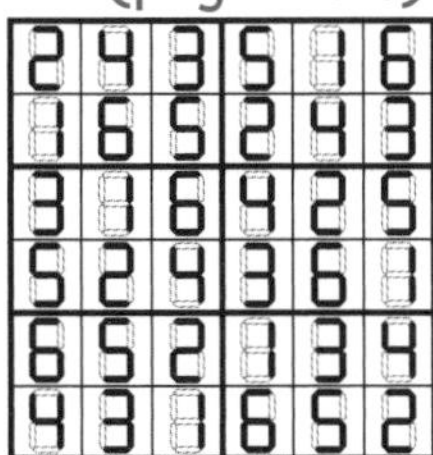

Break the Code (page 104)

Star = 5, Diamond = 3, Circle = 2, and Arrow = 1. The missing number is 9.

Codeword (page 105)

1	2	3	4	5	6	7	8	9	10	11	12	13
F	I	C	A	R	V	U	B	J	L	P	M	N

14	15	16	17	18	19	20	21	22	23	24	25	26
X	S	G	O	Y	K	W	T	D	E	Z	Q	H

International Scramblegram (page 106)

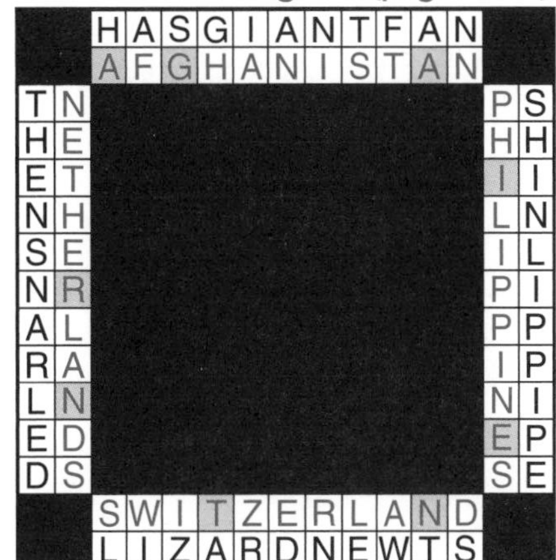

A	G	A	R	N	I	E	T	N
A	R	G	E	N	T	I	N	A

Vex-a-Gon (page 106)

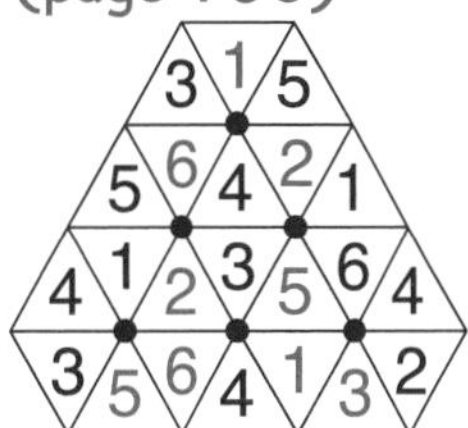

Answers

Digitally Mastered (page 107)

6	2	8	■
3	4	5	6
3	4	1	2
■	2	3	5

Minesweeper (page 107)

					1		1		
	1	*		1	*	2	*	1	
		1	1	1			2		
								*	
	*	1	1	*	1				1
	1								
			1		1				
1				*				1	
*	1				2	1		*	1
1					1	*	2		

The Yellow-Brick Road (page 108)

"If I were to ask the other person which road leads to the city of truth, what would they tell me?" If the liar tells us the truth-teller would say to take the red road, we know that we should take the green road. If the truth-teller tells us the liar would tell is to take the red road, he's telling the truth taking the red road would be a lie. We should do the opposite of what we're told, regardless of who we ask.

Cluster (page 108)

T-Cubed Rectangles (page 109)

Images B and C form a cube when folded.

Familial Sequence (page 109)

Z. The Marx Brothers: Chico, Harpo, Groucho, Gummo, Zeppo

Petal Puzzle (pages 110–111)

Calcu-doku (page 111)

5	6	3	1	2	4
6	2	5	4	3	1
3	5	1	6	4	2
1	4	2	3	5	6
4	3	6	2	1	5
2	1	4	5	6	3

Black Diamonds (page 112)

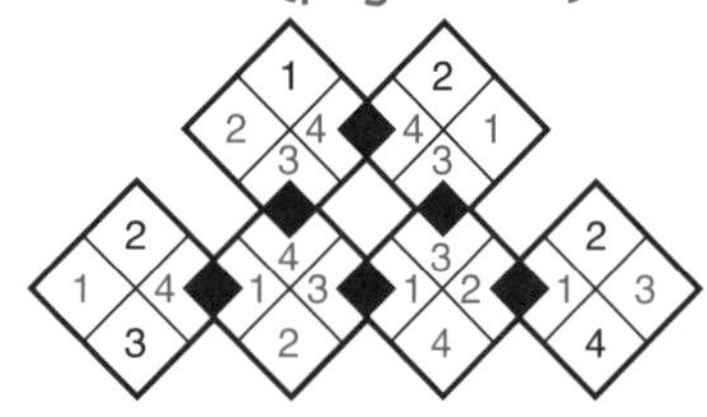

XOXO (page 112)

						X	O						
					O	X	X	X	O				
			X	O	X	O	O	O	X	X			
		X	O	X	X	O	X	O	O	O	X	X	
	O	X	O	X	O	O	X	O	O	X	O	O	
X	O	O	O	X	O	X	O	X	X	X	O	X	X
O	X	X	X	O	X	X	X	O	X	X	X	O	O
X	O	X	X	O	O	O	X	O	X	O	O	O	X
X	O	O	O	X	O	X	X	O	O	O	X	O	X
O	X	X	X	O	O	X	O	X	X	O	X	X	
	O	O	X	O	X	X	O	O	X	X	X	O	
		X	O	O	X	O	X	X	O	O	O	X	O
		X	O	X	X	X	O	O	X				

Word Columns (page 113)

Scotty: "She's all yours, sir. All systems are automated and ready. A chimpanzee and two trainees could run her!" Kirk: "Thank you, Mr. Scott, I'll try not to take that personally." (Star Trek)

Red, White, Blue, and Green (page 114)

G	R	R	W	B	B	G	W
W	G	B	B	G	R	R	W
W	B	W	G	R	G	B	R
R	B	G	R	W	W	B	G
R	W	G	R	B	B	W	G
G	W	B	B	R	W	G	R
B	G	W	G	W	R	R	B
B	R	R	W	G	G	W	B

Kakuro (page 115)

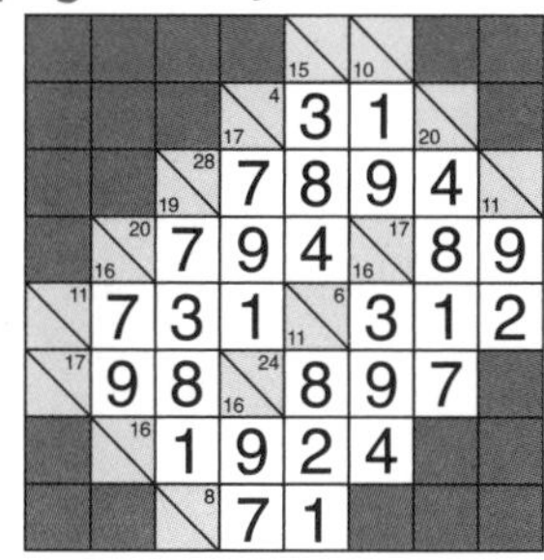

Fitting Words (page 115)

F	A	N	C	Y
E	X	I	L	E
E	L	B	O	W
T	E	S	T	S

Cross-Math (page 116)

5	+	7	×	2	=	24
×		+		+		
3	+	4	-	1	=	6
+		-		×		
9	-	6	×	8	=	24
=		=		=		
24		5		24		

Liar's Logic! (page 116)

The liars are C and E. If C were telling the truth, E would have to be as well, and A, B, and D would have to be lying (as B and D contradict C, and A agrees with B), and this would be too many liars. By such a process of elimination it becomes evident that the ones telling the truth are A, B, and D. We can be sure of everyone's names.

Mixed-up Marriages (page 117)

	Groom 1st	Groom 2nd	Bride 1st	Bride 2nd
1	Eddie	Kite	Nina	Tallis
2	Bill	James	Rosie	Wells
3	Abe	Goliath	Pauline	Underwood
4	Fred	Holderness	Olive	Stephens
5	Doug	Idi	Alice	Yates
6	Colin	Leonard	Minnie	Vitori

Hamster Treadmill (page 118)

The needle will turn clockwise

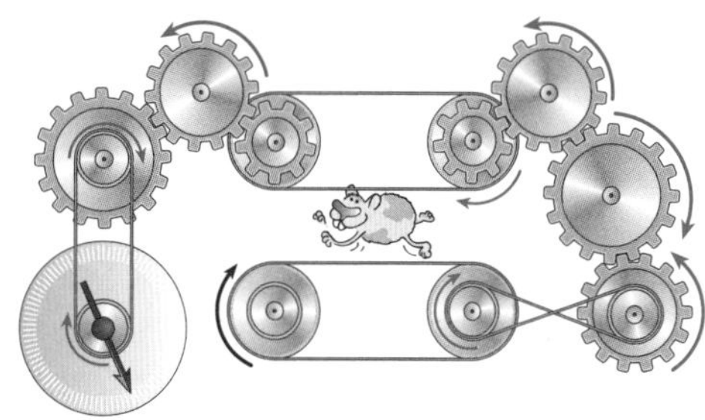

Arrow Web (page 119)

⇨	⇩	⬇	⬂	⇦	⬃	⇩
⇩	⇩	⬂	⬊	⬇	⬃	⇩
⇨	⬊	⬃	⬀	⬃	⇦	⇦
⇨	⬂	⇨	⇧	⇧	⬋	⇦
⬈	⇧	⬆	⬆	⬈	⬆	⬃
⇧	⬀	⇨	⇨	⬀	⬉	⬁
⬀	⇧	⬁	⬈	⬁	⇦	⬅

Circular Memory (Parts I and II) (pages 119–120)

D

Spell Math! (page 120)

Six + seven = thirteen

Answers

Codeword (page 121)

1	2	3	4	5	6	7	8	9	10	11	12	13
G	N	M	A	H	Y	B	O	C	F	T	U	E

14	15	16	17	18	19	20	21	22	23	24	25	26
J	R	K	P	W	V	L	X	Z	S	I	Q	D

Sudoku (page 122)

5	3	1	7	2	8	9	4	6
4	6	8	1	5	9	7	2	3
9	2	7	6	4	3	5	8	1
1	9	2	3	8	5	4	6	7
3	7	5	4	6	1	8	9	2
8	4	6	2	9	7	1	3	5
6	5	4	9	1	2	3	7	8
2	8	3	5	7	4	6	1	9
7	1	9	8	3	6	2	5	4

Age Quandary (page 122)

Combined age in 12 years = 94; 4 × 12 = 48, therefore, combined age now is 94 − 48 = 46; In 5 years from now the combined age will be 46 + 20 (4 × 5) = 66.

Find It (page 123)

Beverages: coffee, cola, tea; Countries: Belgium, Bolivia, Brazil; Characters: Harry, Hermione, Ron; Strong winds: mistral, Santa Ana, simoom; Dairy: cheese, cream, yogurt

Hashi (page 124)

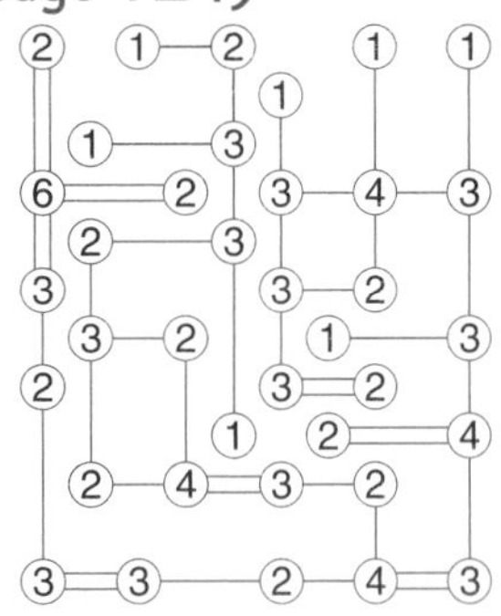

Royal Conundrum (page 125)

A prince. Add an "s" and you get princes, add another "s" and you get princess.

Crypto-Logic (page 125)

FIENDISH. 2F = 5D. $F + \frac{2}{5}F + 3 = X$. So $1\frac{2}{5}F + 3 = 2F$, and $\frac{3}{5}F = 3$. So F = 5. X is 10, and D is 2. Therefore I is 4, and U is - 1, M is - 3, and N is 3. H is therefore 6, and so S must be 8.

Code-doku (page 126)

I	C	D	O	E	U	N	T	A
N	T	U	I	A	C	O	E	D
O	A	E	N	T	D	U	I	C
U	I	A	C	N	E	T	D	O
D	O	N	A	U	T	I	C	E
T	E	C	D	I	O	A	N	U
A	N	O	E	C	I	D	U	T
E	D	T	U	O	N	C	A	I
C	U	I	T	D	A	E	O	N

EDUCATION

1-2-3 (page 126)

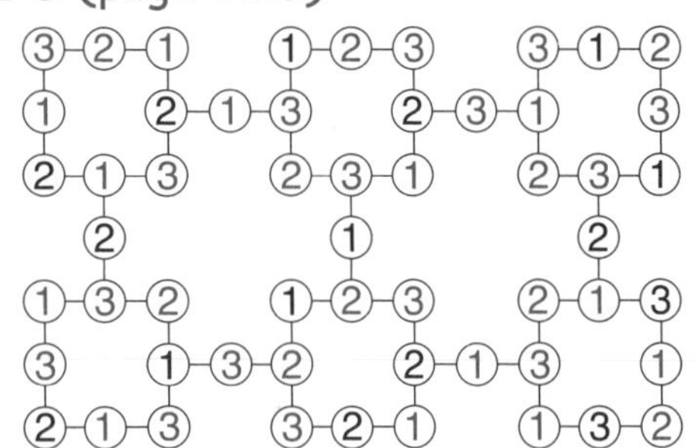

Try Your Luck (page 127)

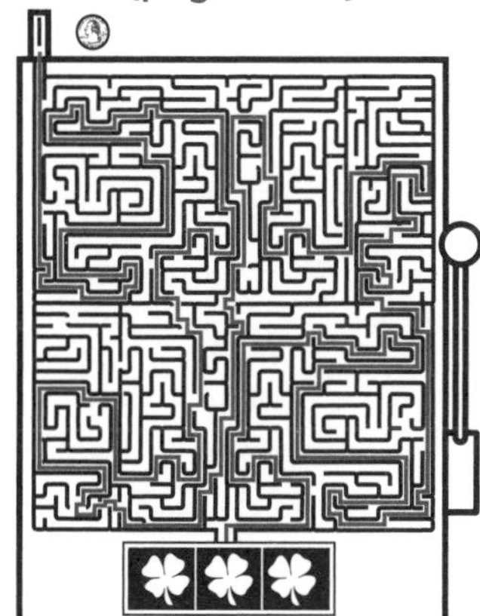

Star Power (page 128)

6	1	7	3	1					
3	★	4	★	6	2	4	8	2	
8	5	2	5	8	★	7	★	1	
1	★	3	★	1	3	5	6	3	5
4	6	7	4	6	1	★	4	★	2
	8	★	5	★	7	2	8	1	7
	3	1	2	8	3	★	6	★	2
					1	4	5	3	4

Cross Sums (page 129)

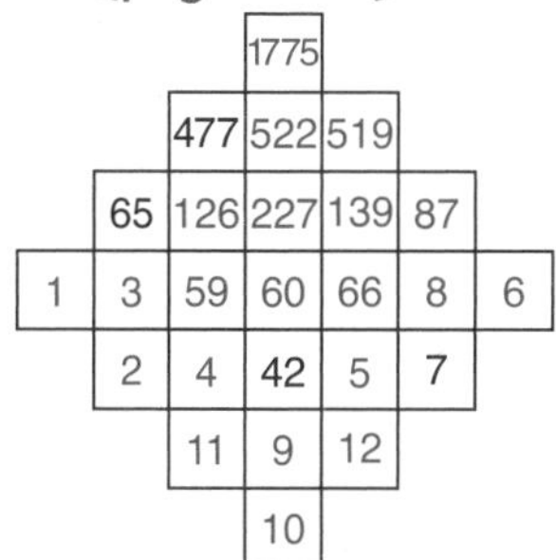

Battle Boats (page 129)

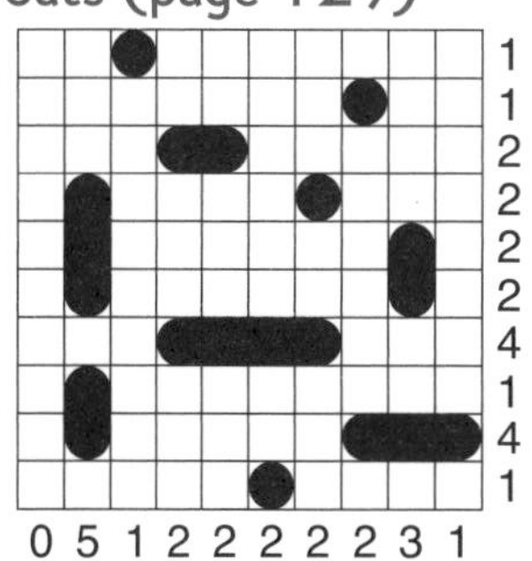

Be Prepared to Solve This (pages 130–131)

Leftover letters spell: The current total number of merit badges is 121.

Fences (page 131)

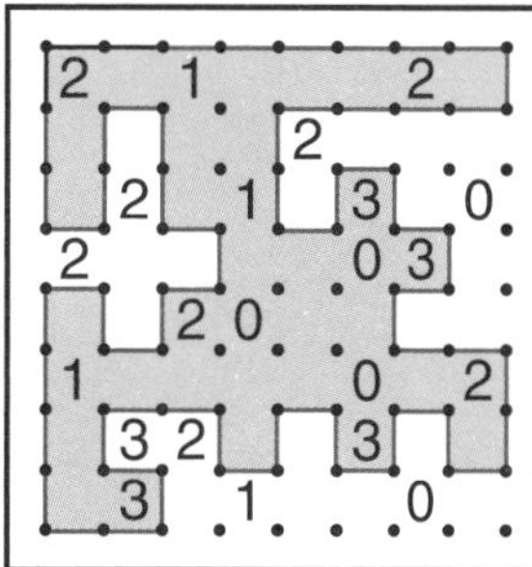

Snake Shapes (page 132)

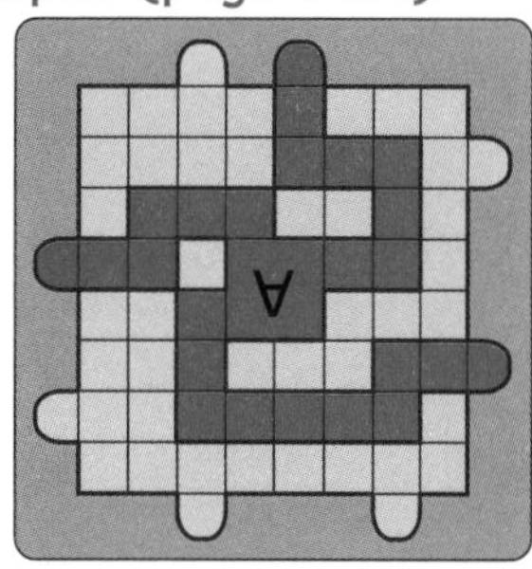

Answers

Odd-Even Logidoku (page 133)

3	1	7	8	5	6	9	4	2
9	2	6	1	7	4	5	3	8
4	8	5	9	2	3	6	1	7
6	4	2	7	9	5	3	8	1
1	3	9	6	8	2	7	5	4
5	7	8	4	3	1	2	9	6
8	5	1	2	6	9	4	7	3
2	9	4	3	1	7	8	6	5
7	6	3	5	4	8	1	2	9

Word Ladder (page 133)

OPINE, spine, spite, spike, spoke, spore, STORE

Alien Mutations (page 134)

A to quadruped; B add antennae; C body circle; D body square; E head circle; F to biped; G remove front appendages; H add antennae; I remove antennae; J remove rear appendages; K add front appendages; L head circle; M head square; N head circle; O add rear appendages; P to quadruped

Word Jigsaw (page 135)

Mastermind (page 135)

13098

Clapboard (pages 136-137)

Grid Fill (page 138)

A	R	C	H	E	R
S	L	I	G	H	T
O	N	T	I	M	E
S	P	A	R	T	A
C	O	O	K	I	E
A	R	R	E	S	T
T	A	M	A	L	E

Poetry in Motion (page 139)

Orange, silver, and purple do not have any words that rhyme with them in the English language.

Dissection (page 139)

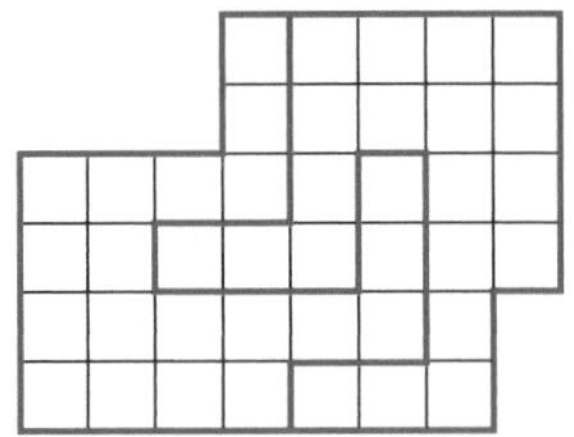

Cross Count (page 140)

9 i	4 m	7 p	1 s	21
3 c	6 o	1 a	3 l	13
5 e	9 r	9 i	5 e	28
9 r	5 e	5 n	4 d	23
26	24	22	13	

Twenty-four Jumble (page 140)

$3 \times 8 \div 6 \times 5 + 4 = 24$

College Baseball by Alpha Sleuth™ (page 141)

ROUNDING

THIRD

XOXO (page 142)

			O		X			X					
		X	X	O	O	O	X	X	O				
	X	O	O	X	X	X	O	O	X	O	X		
X	O	X	X	O	O	O	X	O	X	O	O		
	O	X	O	O	X	X	X	O	X	X	O	X	
X	O	O	O	X	X	X	O	X	O	X	O	O	
	X	X	O	O	O	X	O	O	O	X	X	O	X
	O	X	X	X	O	O	O	X	X	O	X	O	
		X	O	O	O	X	X	X	O	O		X	
		O		X	X		O		O				

Sum Puzzle (page 143)

Answers may vary.

2	1	4	5	7	6	3	2
4	4	1	6	2	1	9	3
4	2	5	1	4	8	2	4
1	5	7	2	5	3	5	2
2	6	1	3	6	4	2	6
7	3	4	1	2	5	1	7
9	1	6	7	1	1	3	2
1	8	2	5	3	2	5	4

Movie Title and Director Cryptogram (page 143)

1. *North by Northwest*: Alfred Hitchcock; 2. *The Shining*: Stanley Kubrick; 3. *Citizen Kane*: Orson Welles; 4. *Raging Bull*: Martin Scorsese

Kakuro (page 144)

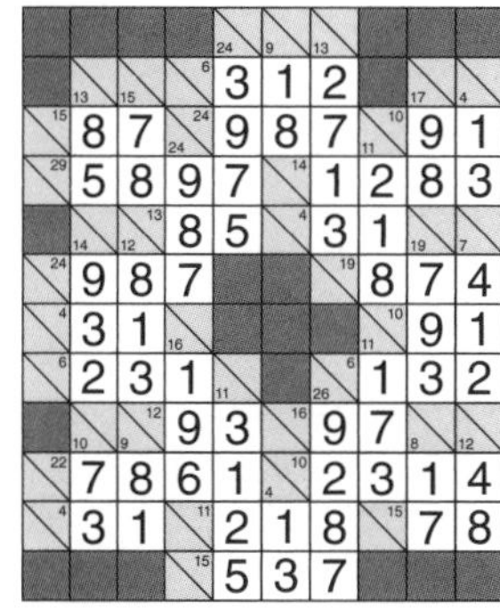

Hobby Horse (page 145)

A. astronomy; B. CELEBRITY; C. needlepoint; D. upholstery

Marbles (page 145)

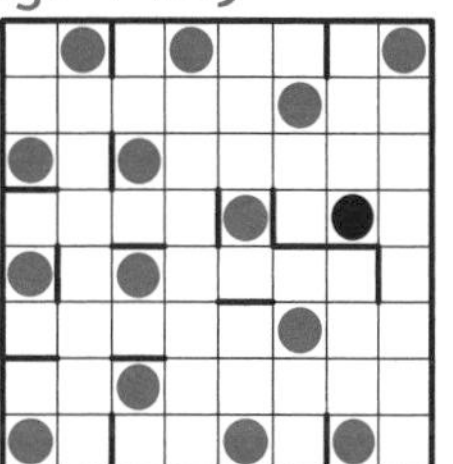

Rhyme Time (page 146)

1. hot lot; 2. wet set; 3. hear deer; 4. bold hold; 5. line nine; 6. ring thing; 7. Gaza plaza; 8. grabs slabs; 9. skate great; 10. pound ground; 11. shrill trill; 12. resort report; 13. chance glance; 14. history mystery; 15. winter splinter

Sudoku (page 147)

1	3	7	9	2	4	6	5	8
8	2	5	6	7	3	1	4	9
4	9	6	5	8	1	2	7	3
3	5	1	2	9	7	4	8	6
7	6	2	4	3	8	9	1	5
9	4	8	1	6	5	7	3	2
2	7	4	3	5	9	8	6	1
5	1	9	8	4	6	3	2	7
6	8	3	7	1	2	5	9	4

Symbol Value (page 147)

■ = 20

□ = 12

○ = 16

● = 24

Double Goalposts (pages 148–149)

Answers

Get It Straight (page 150)

Elevator Words (page 151)

1. SWITCH gear; 2. gear wheel; 3. wheel horse; 4. horse trade; 5. trade secret; 6. secret service; 7. service ENTRANCE

Famous Anagrams (page 151)

A. Rene Descartes; B. Noam Chomsky; C. HENRI MATISSE; D. Immanuel Kant

Hungry Scramblegram (page 152)

R	A	N	R	U	F	F	T	R	E	K
F	R	A	N	K	F	U	R	T	E	R

B	G
I	I
G	N
G	G
A	E
R	R
D	B
E	R
N	E
E	A
R	D

T	A
A	L
G	I
L	T
I	T
A	L
T	E
E	G
L	A
L	L
E	E

P	E	P	P	E	R	M	I	N	T	S
P	I	M	P	S	R	E	P	E	N	T

F	A	K	E	E	B	T	E	S
B	E	E	F	S	T	E	A	K

Flip the Cards (page 152)

D. We don't need to turn all the 7s, since we just need to know that no other numbers have Fs on them, not that all 7s do.

ABCD (page 153)

C	A	C	D	A	D	C	D	A
D	B	D	C	D	B	D	B	D
A	C	B	A	B	D	B	A	C
D	B	C	D	C	B	C	D	B
A	C	B	A	B	C	A	B	C
D	B	D	C	A	D	B	D	A

Logidoku (page 154)

3	7	9	1	4	6	8	2	5
8	2	6	5	7	9	4	1	3
4	5	1	2	3	8	9	7	6
7	6	4	9	5	2	3	8	1
1	9	3	6	8	4	7	5	2
5	8	2	3	1	7	6	4	9
2	3	7	4	6	1	5	9	8
9	4	5	8	2	3	1	6	7
6	1	8	7	9	5	2	3	4

Mindsweeper (page 154)

*	2						*		*
2	*			1		2	2	2	1
		2	2	*		*	2		
	2		*	2		*		1	
*		*	2			*		*	1
*	5	2	2		3	*	*	2	
*	*	2		*	2	2		1	
*	*	2						2	
	3					1	*		*
1	*	2	*	1		1	2	*	2

Acrostic (page 155)

"Once we are destined to live out our lives in the prison of our mind, our duty is to furnish it well."

—Peter Ustinov

A. Peter Ustinov; B. souvenir; C. Houdini; D. freeloader; E. tousle; F. chowder; G. deformity; H. tuition; I. Wilson; J. insult

Digital Sudoku (page 156)

3	2	5	1	6	4
6	4	1	2	5	3
4	6	2	5	3	1
5	1	3	6	4	2
1	3	6	4	2	5
2	5	4	3	1	6

Marbles (page 156)

Plan Ahead (Parts I and II) (pages 157–158)

1. May; 2. Mom and Dad's 35th anniversary; 3. 2:30; 4. Kate and Tony; 5. Business appointment with Cheesy Corporation at 11:30; 6. Thursday the 20th, at 12:30; 7. Sales conference; 8. Helena at 4:15; 9. Bowling; 10. Dave

Say What? (page 158)

"It was high counsel that I had once heard given to a young person, "'Always do what you are afraid to do.'" —Ralph Waldo Emerson

Word Columns (page 159)

"There are many in this old world of ours who hold that things break about even for all of us. I have observed for example that we all get the same amount of ice. The rich get it in the summertime and the poor get it in the winter."

Alien Mutations (page 160)

A body circle; B head circle; C add antennae; D remove antennae; E to biped; F body square; G remove rear appendages; H head circle; I head square; J remove front appendages; K add rear appendages; L to biped; M to quadruped; N to biped; O ad front appendages; P body circle

Battle Boats (page 161)

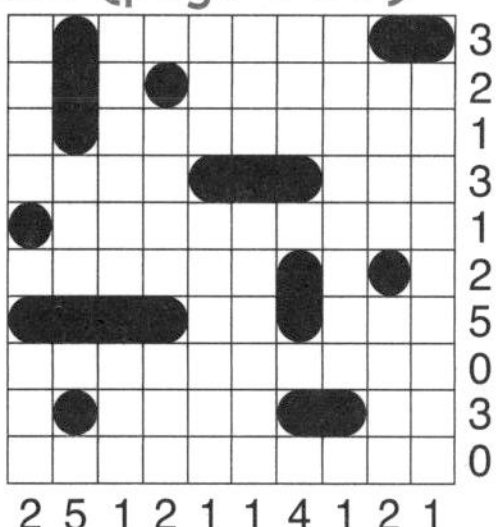

Red, White, Blue, and Green (page 162)

B	R	W	G	B	W	G	R
G	W	R	R	W	B	B	G
B	G	R	W	G	R	W	B
R	W	G	B	G	R	W	B
R	G	B	G	W	B	R	W
W	B	W	B	R	G	G	R
G	B	G	R	B	W	R	W
W	R	B	W	R	G	B	G

Cross Sums (page 163)

			995			
		280	296	301		
	59	69	118	80	65	
11	2	34	29	38	8	10
	12	4	17	5	9	
		1	3	7		
			6			

Answers

Crypto-Logic (page 163)

NUANCED. U + A = 5. So X is 10. So N is 5. The only values which will make 5 when added, which are present in the encrypted sequence of letters, are 2 and 3, which are the values of A and of U. Therefore D is 1 and C is 9.

Mastermind (page 164)

70954

Window Boxes (page 164)

The total number of section squares and windows in each tower corresponds with the position of the letter directly beneath it in the alphabet.

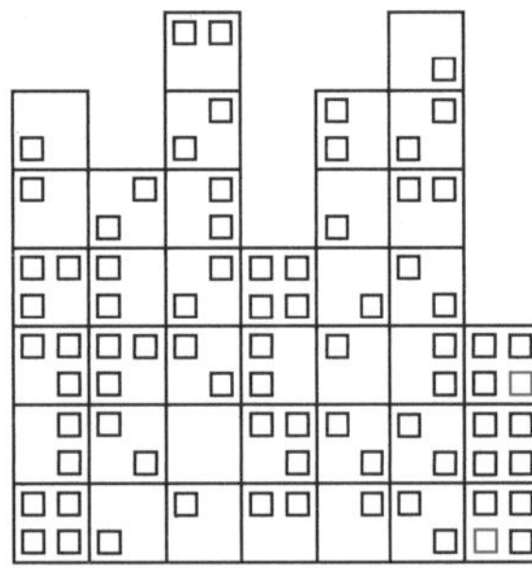

Snake Shapes (page 165)

INDEX

Continued on page 192

Index

Language

Continued from page 191

Logic

Mazes

Memory

Problem Solving

Spatial Reasoning

Spatial Visualization

Sudoku

Visual Logic

Visual Search

Word Searches